T0123409

CLAIM THE WOMAN YOU ARE MEANT TO BE!

10 KEYS TO BREAK THROUGH LIMITING SELF-EXPECTATIONS

CAROLE ROSE

BALBOA.
PRESS

A DIVISION OF HAY HOUSE

Scripture taken from the King James Version of the Bible.

Balboa Press books may be ordered through booksellers or by contacting:

Balboa Press
A Division of Hay House
1663 Liberty Drive
Bloomington, IN 47403
www.balboapress.com
1 (877) 407-4847

Print information available on the last page.

ISBN: 978-1-9822-0486-0 (sc)
ISBN: 978-1-9822-0488-4 (hc)
ISBN: 978-1-9822-0487-7 (e)

Library of Congress Control Number: 2018906231

Balboa Press rev. date: 05/30/2018

CONTENTS

Foreword vii

Dedication ix

What Carole's Students Are Saying xi

Introduction xiii

    Claim The Woman You Are Meant To Be" xiii

Key #1 1

    Define Success In Your Own Terms 1

Key #2 19

    Understand The Universal Laws 19

Key #3 37

    Decode How Your Brain Works 37

Key #4 59

    Get To Know Yourself 59

Key #5 118

    Let Your Values Guide Your Life 118

Key #6 137

    Heal Your Money Story And Invite Abundance 137

Key #7 177

    Your Value Based Passion And Purpose 177

Key #8 185

    Dare To Dream 185

Key # 9 203

    Change A Belief ~ Change Your Life 203

KEY #10 232

    Never Give Up 232

CONCLUSION 253

FOREWORD

A woman's guide to breaking through limiting self-expectations so she can become all she was meant to be, step up to her divine passion, and create financial security doing what she loves to do.

Carole Rose, one of the leaders in the human potential movement, has given women 10 Keys to change their lives. And, Carole is a living testimony to the transformation that any woman can achieve. She openly shares her life story of abuse, chaos, confusion and depression that resulted from unconscious beliefs that were sabotaging her happiness and success.

You will be inspired at just how simple it is to go from victim to victor, from, "I'm not enough!" to "I'm perfect, just the way I am!"

Carole has a gift for translating universal principles and spiritual laws into down-to-earth concepts that you can easily applied to your own life. Carole is colorful to say the least. She will have you in tears one minute and laughing the next.

Let Carole show you that you are so much greater than anything you have ever thought you could be. No matter what you've been through in your life, regardless of shame, regret and paralyzing fear, you can find happiness and success. You can find love. You can attain financial freedom.

I guarantee, you'll have a hard time putting this book down.

Kathleen Ronald
Founder -Speaktacular

DEDICATION

I dedicate this book to my daughter Heidi Webb who inherited many of my limiting self-expectations, suffered heartache and went on to create an astonishing life anyway.

You inspire me!

Thank you for your unwavering support and encouragement. We did it Baby!

WHAT CAROLE'S STUDENTS ARE SAYING

"…..insightful, informative and inspirational. Carole Rose shows you ways to reconstruct your thinking and attitudes towards money and life decisions. *If you are experiencing concerns and questions about money and/or life transitions or feel stuck in your daily routine*, attend a 'Break Through Your Success Blocks' workshop and experience the amazing difference for yourself!" -Bonnie Rogers

"Since I attended your seminar, *my life just seems to be effortlessly going in the right direction.* So many things have changed in the way I perceive things, and react to life. The old me was a nervous wreck all the time. It seems I was always frazzled about something. I often felt like I was swimming upstream against the current. Now it's as if my life just flows right along." -Tracy Adair

"After one coaching session with Carole I became hopeful again. Through Carole's NLP coaching, I immediately began creating new possibilities for a prosperous and inspiring future thereby increasing my optimism and my creative vibration. This increased vibration transferred to my husband and in 3 weeks he was hired for a wonderful position where he aced out 3,000 applicants. Carole's coaching demonstrated to me the power behind her wisdom and skill as a transformational practitioner. **It was a magical experience, with real life results, which changed my limiting beliefs and**

my life! I am grateful for Carole and her dedication to helping others create new possibilities in their lives" - Elizabeth Jolissaint

"Carole is the Universal Mother of true transformation. She is honest and warm and truly believes in empowering women. Carole has changed my life in only 48 hours and I will be better for the rest of my life."- Myette A. Millione

"Carole is truly masterful at her speaking and breakthrough work. The principles Carole uses for her Wealth Mentorship can be used in ANY area of your life. During one of her seminars, I uncovered and proceeded to release a limiting belief that was CORE to my happiness and success. Carole is a living, breathing example of her work too. She is very honest and committed to becoming the best she can be personally and professionally. I feel very lucky to know Carole is on my team when I need her!" - Maurine Xavier

INTRODUCTION

CLAIM THE WOMAN YOU ARE MEANT TO BE"

Are you living up to your potential? Do you ever feel like you are not being your authentic self? Do you wonder if you are lovable, just the way you are? Do you sabotage your success or happiness? If so, join the crowd, most women doubt their own worth. Many are living out expectations that someone else had for them, in love and relationships, and in business and financial achievement. Then, we wonder why we feel anxious and discontent.

I was raised to be a homemaker, nothing else. I was taught that men only loved and married docile, subservient women, like my mother and June Cleaver. But, I didn't possess those lovable qualities. I was headstrong and willful, assertive and aggressive. Still, all I ever wanted, was to get married and be a homemaker. I tried to be domestic. I married at 14, then 16, 18, 25, 32 and 50. (You might call me a serial bride). I blamed my husbands for the first 5 failed marriages. It was their fault I wasn't contented and fulfilled. I had no idea, that my soul was craving far more challenge and mental stimulation than tedious housework provided for me. How could I know that my authentic calling is teaching? How could it be? I was dumb. After all, I only had a ninth-grade education.

Even after impressive successes, and being acknowledged in Who's Who of American Women and the World Who's Who of Women; despite being hired for over $300,000 a year, a part of me felt like a fraud. Unconsciously, I'd think; 'This isn't who I was meant to be. I'm supposed to be working at Ross or married and baking cookies'. Consequently, that subconscious belief caused me to continually sabotage my success. That's how I became an expert. I had to fix myself.

If you learn the 10 Keys in this book, and do the work, which I call, 'Transformation Explorations' you can claim the woman you are meant to be. Almost every woman who came to my workshops doubted their own self-worth. They wanted to do more with their life but didn't believe they had what it takes. Some women wanted love but stayed in abusive relationships. This too, resulted from low self-esteem. Women are not raised to see assertiveness and ambition as a feminine quality, although thankfully, that is changing. Those qualities were definitely discouraged in me growing up. It takes intense work to break through decades of programing, so we can claim the woman we are meant to be.

I promise, you are going to discover more about yourself, and your loved ones, than you ever thought possible. Part of the work may bring up painful memories and perhaps, even feelings of guilt and shame. It did for me. When that happens, take a deep breath and say:

"I deeply and completely love and accept myself. I deeply and completely love and accept myself."

That sentence has helped me find forgiveness. And, without forgiveness, of ourselves and others, we cannot find self-love, and, without self-love, we cannot claim the woman we are meant to be. So, I recommend that, as you do the work, you repeat that often. Believe me, you'll need it.

The "Law of attraction" is irrefutable. Our unconscious expectations cause us to create self-fulfilling prophecies. In fact, it's impossible not to act consistent with our expectations. If you want to know what your unconscious self-expectations are, just look around you. Are you constantly struggling with finances? Chances are, you created it. Are you in love with someone who cheats on you? You chose it. Are you 50 pounds over-weight? Part of you wants it. If you don't like what you see in your life, change it. I'll give you the know-how and the tools to transform your life; every bit of it. From your love life to your business life. I know the pain and suffering our lack of self-worth creates. It is my purpose in life to help women break through limiting self-expectations, so they can become the woman they are meant to be, step up to their divine purpose, create abundance, and most importantly, learn to love themselves so others can love them too.

ARE YOU PLAYING A ROLE THAT IS NOT THE AUTHENTIC YOU? Have you been sabotaging your wealth and success, and maybe love? Here are a few symptoms:
- Not charging what you're worth
- You're good at what you do, but wealth & success still elude you
- You feel frustrated and discontented
- Not collecting money that is owed you.
- Attracting abusive partners or employers
- Self-sabotage
- Just not playing full out
- The '*fraud syndrome*'- Not feeling worthy.

Let me show you how to
- ALIGN YOUR VISION WITH YOUR VALUES
- KNOW THAT YOU'RE LOVABLE AND PERFECT just the way you are.

- Have the COURAGE TO TAKE CONTROL OF YOUR OWN DESTINY, whether that means leaving a dysfunctional relationship or job, or stepping up to your purpose so you can share your gifts with the world
- Become FINANCIALLY INDEPENDENT DOING WHAT YOU LOVE.
- Find your PASSION AND PURPOSE and start living the life you deserve.

I'd like you to think of me as your wise old Aunt. You are one of my wonderful nieces. Let me know about your transformation.

To Your Fabulous Transformation

With Affection

Aunt Carole

DEFINE SUCCESS IN YOUR OWN TERMS

PART I: FOUR REQUISITES FOR SUCCESS

To claim the woman you are meant to be, you need to have a clear definition of success. But first, let me simplify what it takes to succeed, at anything. From all the things I've learned about 'succeeding' from books, workshops, mentors, and my own experience, I decided there are really only four essential requisites to success. That doesn't mean they are the only things, but without these four, you'll never achieve the goal. I think you will agree wholeheartedly. Maybe this will help you to see why you have been struggling with some area of your life. Maybe you'll have an "Ah ha!" moment and stop beating yourself up for not excelling when you know you have the ability. The rest of the book is how to master the four requisites. That's the part that took many years for me. I hope an amazing transformation will happen for you. For years, I felt bad about myself because I kept failing– in love and business. I now know it doesn't have to be that way.

$$D + B + P + P = SUCCESS$$

1. YOU'VE GOT TO DREAM

If you'd like to be happily married, lose weight, quit smoking, or succeed in business, first you must dare to dream that you can have it. When a talk show host interviewed the famous billionaire, H.L. Hunt, he posed this question, "Mr. Hunt, if you could give our viewing audience one tip that would make them more successful, what would it be?" Without hesitation, Hunt replied, "If you want to be more successful, first decide what it is you want." You may 'want' to get married and live happily ever after, but have you made a list of exactly what that would look like? You say you dream of being a business success, but exactly what does that mean. Does it mean you must become a billionaire to feel successful? If your dream is to get fit, does that mean you need to have six-pack abs? You'll be clarifying your goals and dreams in later chapters.

2. BELIEF TRUMPS DREAMS

Our beliefs and self-expectations create our destiny. You must BELIEVE that happy marriages, losing weight or business success are possible-in general and for you personally. I mean, believe it subconsciously. I would've sworn I wanted to be rich, but those damn unconscious beliefs sabotaged me.

If you set a goal to earn $100,000 but you don't believe you can do it or that it is not possible, you will not get it. Or, if you do, you will quickly lose it. You've probably heard that lottery winners invariably go broke within a very short time. Yes, they mismanage the money, but 'why' do they mismanage it? Because being rich is incongruent with who they think they are. You can't escape it.

> "One person with a belief is equal to ninety-nine who have only interests." John Stuart Mill https://www.brainyquote.com/quotes/quotes/j/johnstuart132425.html

Belief is very powerful. Here's a great example. When Kathy Miller was 16, she was struck by a car with such an impact that it knocked her out of her shoes. She was left with a twisted leg and foot and severe brain damage. The doctor told her parents that she probably wouldn't live, but if by some miracle, she survived, she would be a human vegetable for the rest of her life. Kathy Miller's mother refused to accept that prognosis. In fact, she gave orders that no one, not the doctors, nurses or attendants, were allowed to utter one negative word in Kathy's room. As Kathy lay there in a coma, her mother played positive thinking tapes by Dr. Norman Vincent Peale and Robert Schuller and she kept telling Kathy, "Every day, in every way, you're getting better and better." For months, she laid curled up in the fetal position and she wasted away to a mere 50 pounds. Did the positive thinking help? Well, 10 months later, Kathy Miller entered the north bank 10,000-meter run, and although 2900 entrants had crossed the finish line before her, there were still 50 stragglers left behind her. She lived and fully recovered. What do you suppose the outcome would have been if while Kathy was laying there, supposedly unconscious, hearing comments like, "Oh, poor Kathy she's going to die any minute. She'll never walk again."? I've also heard that Elvis Presley had a self-fulfilling prophecy that he would die in his early 40s like his mother had. Clearly his prescription drug abuse and lifestyle brought about his untimely death but, what would have been his fate had he prophesied it living to 90?

Here's one more example that is simply awesome. In a recent research done on schizophrenics the beliefs they held about their alter personality were so strong that even physical characteristics changed. The researchers were astonished to see eye color literally change from brown to blue, birthmarks disappear and reappear. Even diseases such as diabetes and high blood pressure would come and go with the various personas.

What do you believe is possible? Are you a fan of Dancing with the Stars? If so, you'll remember Terra Jolé, the movie star and producer. She was born with dwarfism and, at 36 years old, stands just 4' tall. She is most recognized for the reality television series, *Little Women:* She has proven that people with her handicap can do just about anything. She obviously, didn't have parents like mine who assumed that my minor handicap limited me to cleaning house.

> "If thou canst believe, all things are possible to him
> that believeth."
>
> Jesus – Mark 9:23

3. PASSION & PURPOSE

In "Think and Grow Rich", Hill states that the real secret to succeeding is listed about 13 times in the book. I had to re-read the book a few times to find the secret. It is 'burning desire'. Successful people have a desire so intense that they can't help but succeed. But someone might ask, "Where do you get the burning desire?" I find there are two answers to that question. First is 'reasons'. People can do the most amazing things if they have enough reasons. Suppose you want a new car but the payment would be $500 a month and you can't afford it. You might think it is impossible to earn that extra money. Or not worth the sacrifice. Now, suppose your child needed a lifesaving treatment that was going to cost $900 a month, could you find a way to earn it? Of course, you could, and you would! But maybe your reason for succeeding does not create such an urgency or burning desire. There is another, even better way, to ignite the fire, find your 'passion' and 'purpose'.

I don't care how many talents and skills you have, unless you are truly passionate about it you will never be great at what you do. Even if you haven't discovered it yet, you have a divine purpose for your life. Mark Twain said, "The two most important days in your life are the day you were born and the day you find out why." Most people never do find their 'why'. I found my purpose by accident when I accepted the challenge to train Realtors when I was 31. I was a natural! I had high school and college teachers take my class and tell me what a great teacher I was. I had no clue what I was doing right. I also taught at college and wrote a course on "Effective Real Estate Sales". Imagine, me, with a 9th grade education, a college instructor. Boy, I sure wouldn't have seen that as *'realistic'*. And oh, how I loved It. My teaching evolved into teaching women to live inspiring lives. I would work for free to teach. And, I am right now by donating workshops to disadvantaged women. That is my divine purpose.

I included an entire chapter on finding your passion and purpose. I'll tell you what isn't a divine passion or purpose, money. That's right, the money is only a by-product of following your path. Think about this. For most of us, unless you're an aesthetic, money is inexorably connected to succeeding at our profession. Even if you are fund raising for a cause and give the money away. If you are good at what you do, money will come. But, of course, if like me, you won't allow the money to come, you won't allow the success either. You can't fulfill your destiny without handling the money issue. The chapter, 'Heal Your Money Story and Invite abundance' will be life changing, for everyone. And, it isn't just people with enough of it who need help. Julie, who I coached, had been raised with great wealth in South America. In fact, she was almost royalty in this third world country. She lived in a palace and was surrounded by servants, and guards. You'd think she would demand a man who could maintain her luxurious lifestyle, but she avoided rich men like most of us avoid poor men. Why? Because she had anchored wealth to corruption, deceit, and evil. She believed, unconsciously of course, that "Money is power and power corrupts, absolutely". That was a good belief to change.

4. PERSEVERANCE

One final thing all successful people have in common -- they persevered. Despite all obstacles, despite all defeats and setbacks, they never gave up. It took Wilma Rudolf years to even walk without braces, let alone run. Yet she won the Olympic Gold Medal. Sometimes we are persevering toward a goal that the Universe won't let us have, and that usually turns out to be a good thing. You'll learn more about persevering later and how to go on when the going gets tough.

To keep going, even when there are huge obstacles, fear, and worry, you need to find your burning desire, your passion, your purpose for persevering. If you really believed you could quit smoking or read 2000 words per minute, be happily married or make your fondest dream come true, and, you passionately and congruently want it, wouldn't you persevere? What I mean by 'congruently', is that your subconscious must want the same thing for you.

Remember, when we were about 8 years old we learned to be realistic. Well, I don't think it was very realistic for a black orphan girl in the south to become Oprah. When Lucille Ball was 16 she went to acting school in New York. Her acting coach told her she had no talent. Francine Ward was raised in Harlem and expected to grow up to be a hooker and drug addict. Then, she met someone who believed in her possibilities. She is now a copywrite attorney living a life she never knew was possible. That list goes on and on. If you think about it, most achievements were unrealistic. So, you're going to stop being realistic. I know, there will be people in your life who will say you are crazy, foolish and stupid. Yeah, they are the ones who haven't made it themselves. We all have Naysayers in our lives and in a later chapter I'll tell you how to handle them.

I doubt there was a dry eye in the 'Dancing with the Stars' viewing audience when Val's partner, Victoria Arlen told her story.

When she was eleven she fell ill and was diagnosed with two rare conditions known as transverse myelitis and acute disseminated encephalomyelitis. Either one alone could be fatal. The two, together, in one frail body, seemed like a death sentence. She got weaker and fell into a coma. Doctors held little hope. But, even though Victoria couldn't speak, she heard every word that was said. She knew she wasn't expected to survive very long.

Victoria *decided* she was not going to die. She *believed* she could and would get well. She certainly felt *passionate* about it, and she fought like the devil to live. That *perseverance* slowly paid off. After almost four years, Victoria had enough strength to begin re-learning how to speak, eat, and move.

Two years later, in June 2012, she set records at the 2012 Summer Paralympics US swimming trials, winning four medals: one gold and three silver. In 2015 Victoria joined ESPN as a sportscaster. Now, what was your excuse again? It makes my gimpy arm seem like a flea bite.

TRANSFORMATION EXPLORATION 1: FOUR REQUISITES

How many areas of your life can you apply the four requisites to? Write it down

SUMMARY:

To claim the woman you are meant to be, those four things must be in alignment. It's not about willpower or self-discipline -- that's what you need to do something that you don't want to do, like diet to lose 30 pounds. If you follow your dream you can accomplish amazing, 'unrealistic' things.

So, dare to dream, use the tools in this book to develop belief in yourself, find and follow your divine purpose, and never give up. Simple, right? Well, read on and do the work and it will become simple- not easy, but simple. The rest of the book is 'how to' dare to dream big, develop unwavering belief in yourself and your dream, find your passion and purpose, and get the tools to persevere until you manifest it. (Although, not in that order.) You can do it!

> "Do not think of today's failures, but of the successes that may come tomorrow. You have set yourself a difficult task, but you will succeed if you persevere; and you will find a joy in overcoming the obstacles."

> ~Helen Keller

PART II: WHAT IS SUCCESS?

How will you know when you are successful? Money? If so, how much? Many people measure success by how much money a person has. I sure did. But that is not it. Money may be a byproduct of success, and in some fields, it may even be a measurement of success. However, you can win the lotto and not be a success. You can inherit $10 Million and not be a success. On the other hand, you wouldn't say that Mother Teresa and Gandhi were not successful just because they weren't highly paid, right?

Not surprising, since I started studying personal development in the early 70s, all my early mentors were men. All my business models were also male. But, it turns out, the masculine version of business success is not right for most females. Here's why. From pre-history men have been warriors and hunters. They worked as a team to bring down the Wooley Mammoth, or an enemy clan, but communicated very little. A good thing, since silence was critical. The male who had the most kills, and was the toughest, had the most respect. By natures' plan men are competitive. They want to be the Alpha Male. Winning is all-important to them.

You can hear it in their language. "Go for the jugular", "I killed it!" "Crush the competition." The PBS series, 'The Men Who Built America', was about the handful of billionaires who controlled the nation; J.P. Morgan, John D. Rockefeller, Andrew Carnegie. They were ruthless and greedy. They would do anything necessary to beat the competition. Their attitude was, 'All is fair as long as you win'. They even wanted to bankrupt the competition. Ask a man what he would do with $1,000,000 and he will give you a long list of toys-Ferraris, yachts, jets, and maybe a few assault weapons. That is how Alpha Males measure their success. By his definition, I guess Mother Theresa and Gandhi would've been miserable failures. If the only way you will feel successful is if you have more money than the next guy, then you are probably a man.

Women are very different. From pre-history, we stayed close to the cave taking care of little Neanderthals, so they wouldn't get eaten by a saber tooth tiger. We had to develop communication skills. We had to teach the kids how to interact with others. We are the peacemakers and we want to see everyone win. Masculine model, 'Win at any cost', Feminine way, 'Win-Win'. We know there is enough to share. My husbands (5 & 6) were both astounded that I trained my competition to succeed (Real Estate Trainer, President of local NARI (National Association Remodeling Industry). I gave them all my secrets to be a top producer. Why not? There is enough for all of us.

Women are not motivated by money. Not that we don't want riches. Oh yeah, I want to vacation in Europe, often, drive a luxury car, have a maid. But more than that, we women want to take care of our children and grandchildren, and siblings and parents, and the poor and unfortunate, the world! Right? Ask any woman what she would do with the money if she won the lottery and her answer will start with "I will help someone".

Of course, we want, and need, financial security. Many women's number one fear is that they will become a bag lady. Since I work with homeless women, I can tell you that is a legitimate fear. Roberta had a nice home, job and fancy tea service. She became disabled and is now sleeping on the sidewalk. Yes, ladies, you damn well better put financial security high on your priority list! That is different than getting rich.

So, the first thing to do is define success in your own terms. How will you know you are successful if you are measuring it by someone else's criteria? Here are nineteen things that mean success to women per the Huffington Post survey in 2013.

1. Doing something impactful and loving every minute of it.
2. Finding the good in life's imperfections.
3. Realizing that your contribution to the work is valued, if not by others, by you.
4. Making a difference by teaching others to achieve success.
5. Living and loving fully, without shame and without apology.
6. Promoting a just cause, such as the fight against ethnic profiling.
7. Going to the beach every day!
8. Making your family happy.
9. Playing an active role in achieving gender equality.
10. Having the ability to control your schedule.
11. Being healthy and having a job that helps other women do the same.
12. Having the strength to try, try again-even when you fall flat on your face.
13. Being proud of yourself.

14. Doing your best and being grateful for everything good in your life.
15. Finding a healthy balance between a loving home and a career you enjoy.
16. Having people in your life who can always make you smile.
17. Loving what you do for a living.
18. Knowing that your daughter will be able to stand up for what's right and is not afraid to be herself around others.
19. Learning to be in the moment instead of constantly going, going, going.

While this survey may not have been performed scientifically, it is consistent with what women in my workshops list. As I said, we also want money, but we are motivated by very different needs than men. Keep these in mind when we do the exercise on values.

PART III: ERRONEOUS BELIEFS ABOUT SUCCESS

Through the media, our parents, our associates, religious leaders, and even our educators, we inherit certain erroneous beliefs about what it takes to succeed. Many of these beliefs have gone unquestioned from generation to generation. They are not founded on fact or even necessarily logic, nonetheless most of us never think to challenge them. If Columbus failed to challenge an erroneous belief, we wouldn't be sitting here. When Isaac Newton was asked how he discovered the law of gravity, he responded, "I questioned an axiom." Here are eight beliefs for us to challenge.

1. You need to have a College degree to succeed in this competitive world.
2. Success is sinful.
3. You must work 80 hours a week and sacrifice your family and all that is important to succeed.

4. You must sacrifice your morals and ethics and step on others to reach the top.
5. High achievers were born with special abilities or talents.
6. Success is a matter of luck.
7. I was born in the wrong part of town or I am the wrong color. Therefore, I lack opportunity.
8. I'm too old.

1. YOU NEED TO HAVE A COLLEGE DEGREE

While growing up, it was pounded into my head that you need to finish school if you expect to get a job.

When I began reading books like "Think and Grow Rich" and "Success Through a Positive Mental Attitude", I learned about hundreds of people who became great with far less education than I had. Edison had only three months of school and Ben Franklin two years, Harry Truman had only a high school diploma and Henry Ford only attended school until he was 14. You see, I equated intelligence to education. It is not the same thing. Before there was reading, long before there were even books to read, there were intelligent people. Cochise, the Apache leader, was a brilliant military strategist and a very wise man. This is a good example of changing a belief on the conscious or cognitive level.

I love the story about Henry Ford suing some famous newspaper for libel because; among other things they called Mr. Ford an 'ignoramus'. When the newspapers defense attorney was cross examining Mr. Ford he attempted to prove his ignorance. The attorney asked Mr. Ford a barrage of difficult questions, such as, "In what year was the Revolutionary war fought?" "Who was the general who led a specific battle in the Civil War?" "Who was the 21st president of the United States?" Mr. Ford addressed the judge and jury and responded in this manner, "Your Honor, ladies and gentlemen of the jury, I don't know the answers to those questions. However, I have a row, of buttons on my desk which I can push and have at my immediate disposal people who could answer any of those questions." The judge responded, "This is clearly not indicative of an ignorant man." Ford won the libel suit.

If you believe that you are not smart because you lack education, you are going to miss a lot of opportunities. Just because you don't have a sheepskin, don't think for one moment that you are dumb.

In addition to thinking people with degrees were smarter than me, I thought they were superior. I couldn't imagine holding a conversation with someone so lofty. Now, I have many friends with multiple degrees.

2. SUCCESS IS SINFUL

After my father passed away Mom got a real estate license. I encouraged her to set some goals. She insisted that she was contented without material things and exclaimed in no uncertain terms, "I certainly wouldn't want to be rich!" 20 years later, my sister, vehemently said the exact same words. "I certainly don't want to be rich." It's easy to see how a good Christian might believe that money is sinful. Mom and my sister were certainly convinced that they would not go to heaven if they were rich. I however, thought I wanted to be rich, but, on an unconscious level, I was just as terrified of going to hell. At least Mom and Pat were congruent in their conscious and unconscious beliefs. Something that is critical to success.

The media does its share to add to the misconception that success is evil. The millionaires who died lonely recluses, and the super successful movie stars and politicians who end up alcohol and drug addicts, with their low morals and high divorce rates, get much more publicity than the ones who've been married for 30 or 40 years and are happy and well-adjusted. Scandal sells papers. The media reports what we want to hear and who wants to hear how well someone else is doing while we are just struggling along. We fear that if we get super successful and rich we will turn into Bernie Madoff or Leona Helmsley, The 'Queen of Mean'. It can make you feel self-rightous about your lack of achievement. "I'm not that kind of person". Balderdash!

We (women) would love to feed and clothe the poor and indigent, care for the sick and elderly, donate to the cancer society, MS and the Red Cross. How can we do that if we ain't got nothin' to give? You can't pour water from an empty bucket. Our country can help others and donate billions of dollars to society each year because we are prosperous. Money is not evil. Being rich is not going to change who you are. If you are kind and generous now, being rich will allow you to be even more kind and generous. Think right now what you would do if you had $2Mil. Maybe you would buy a yacht and a Jaguar, or maybe those things aren't even important to you. Perhaps you would like to provide for a college education for your children or grandchildren. Perhaps you'd help your sister get out of an abusive marriage. Perhaps you would donate the entire amount to Haitian refugees. Money or wealth does not have to be the motivator for your success. However, you don't want the money to get in the way of your success as it did mine.

3. YOU MUST WORK HARD AND SACRIFICE YOUR FAMILY TO SUCCEED

The number one misnomer about success is that you have to work hard to get rich and therefore sacrifice family. Sure, we've all heard about people who worked 80 hours a week and sacrificed their family for success, but again, they are not the only ones who succeed. Smart, wealthy and successful people know how to delegate so they can work fewer hours than those of us struggling to survive. They realize that success would seem trivial without their loved ones. A truly successful person is successful in all areas of their lives. If you are not working long, hard hours to make ends meet, then surely you know someone who is.

4. YOU HAVE TO SACRIFICE YOUR MORALS AND ETHICS TO REACH THE TOP

Wrong, wrong! Money is not going to make you something that you are not. If you are an immoral person now, you will have more opportunity to be immoral. If you are a moral person now, you will continue to live a moral life. Did wealth cause Tiger Woods behavior? I think not. Did wealth or greed cause Bernie Madoff to swindle millions of investors? He didn't do it because he needed the money, he did it because he is a sociopath. Did Pres. Kennedy have a long list of sexual liaisons because he was wealthy? Did Al Capone become a criminal because he wanted the wealth, or would he have led a life of crime anyway?

5. HIGH ACHIEVERS WERE BORN WITH MORE ABILITIES OR TALENT THAN ME

No one is born a success, but we are all born with talent. Robert Louis Stevenson said "Worthwhile folks don't just happen you were born worthwhile. You're born with the abilities of becoming worthwhile; your job is to discover and develop the man or woman you ought to be". Most of us only use about 10% of our abilities. If we would maximize that just a little, we would be surprised at all the hidden talent we each possess.

6. SUCCESS IS A MATTER OF LUCK

In speaking of someone else's success there will always be those who would say, "He was lucky". However, those same individuals are quick to take full credit for their own achievements. Mark Twain was once asked whether he believed in luck and he responded "I certainly do. How else can you explain the success of those who detest?" If you thought it was only luck, you wouldn't be reading this book, so I won't belabor this point.

7. I LACK OPPORTUNITY,

There are always those who blame their lack of achievement on lack of opportunity "I came from the wrong part of the country" or "I'm the wrong color or sex", they proclaim. In a recent TV movie, I saw an example of the ultimate lack of opportunity. A man was sentenced to death for murder and while on death row Pres. Wilson commuted his sentence to life in prison. However, he remained in solitary confinement for the rest of his life, forty plus years. Would you say, this man lacked opportunity for achievement? And yet, from his prison cell he began studying mountains of library books and became a self-taught expert on bird pathology and hematology. From his cell, and with the aid of an outside source, he wrote and published a very technical scientific book on the subjects and invented and marketed "Stroud's Specifics", (cures for bird diseases). While in prison he gained recognition as one of the world's foremost experts on birds. As you've guessed by now, his name was Robert Stroud and he was known as "The Bird Man of Alcatraz". Incidentally Robert Stroud only had a third-grade education. We make our own opportunity and luck.

8. I'M TOO OLD, SHORT, FAT, TOO WHATEVER...

Eight out of ten Nobel Prize nominees are over 70. It seems we just get more creative as we get older. Col. Sanders was 65 years old when he founded one of the most successful franchises ever. Grandma Moses was in her 80s when she became a famous artist. George Bernard Shaw didn't sell his first play until he was in his 80s. YOU are not too old!

Hervé Jean-Pierre Villechaize suffered from proportionate dwarfism, likely due to an endocrine disorder. He was only 3'10" tall yet he had a long successful career as an actor. You may remember him from the James Bond movie, 'The Man with the Golden Gun', or perhaps from his role as Tattoo on 'Fantasy Island'. Size didn't hinder him. Nor, did Roseanne Barr let her girth deny her success.

Helen Keller was deaf, dumb, and blind. No opportunity for her to succeed, right? Yet, Keller raised millions for the blind. When he was 30-years-old, my nephew, Ron, was paralyzed from the waist down. It was heartbreaking. However, he called with incredible news last week. He has bought a yacht. He had been dreaming about it for years and he did it! The fellow who sold it to him, couldn't believe it when Ron managed to maneuver himself into the boat that was 9' off the ground. Ron didn't let his limitations squelch his impossible dream. So, what are your excuses?

TRANSFORMATIONAL EXPLORATION 2: DEFINE SUCCESS

- In you journal, write down what success means to you?
- How will you know you are successful? Finish this sentence. "I will know I am successful when…

I want to share two of my favorite definitions of success.

> "Success to me is being able to look yourself square in the face and say that I am proud of the extent to which I have maximized my ability; in my home, my church, my business and my community." Anthony Anthanos- Founder- Anthony's' Pier 4 Restaurants

> "Success to me is finding something that you love to do so much you would do it for free, and then learning to do it so

well people will pay you well to do it." Mary C. Crowley, Founder- Home Interiors, Inc.

SUMMARY:

Now that you've read this, I'm betting you have eliminated at least one erroneous belief that has been preventing you from claiming the woman you are meant to be, at least on a conscious level. You also should have a clearer idea of just what *success* is.

TRANSFORMATION EXPLORATION 3: IDENTIFY YOUR LIMITATIONS

List all the reasons and excuses you have been telling yourself have prevented you from achieving your goals.

It will be interesting to see how it changes after the future chapters, especially after the ones on values and purpose

UNDERSTAND THE UNIVERSAL LAWS

THE LAW OF ATTRACTION

Some people believe that God decides their destiny. In ancient Greece, they had about 2000 gods that were believed to determine everything in life, from rainfall to death. Some people rely on their horoscope or numerology. Still others believe that luck determines their fate. In all cases, their circumstances are completely beyond their control. Yet, some 2500 years ago, Socrates, Confucius and Buddha were teaching that we were not merely living at the whim of the gods. That by using our minds and developing reasoning, we could be the guides to our own destinies instead of helpless pawns.

"All that we are is the result of what we have thought: it is founded on our thoughts and made up of our thoughts. If a man speaks or acts with an evil thought, suffering follows him as the wheel follows the hoof of the beast that draws the wagon.... If a man speaks or acts with a good thought, happiness follows him like a shadow that never leaves him." Gautama Buddha

Jesus put it this way, "As a man thinketh in his heart, so is he." Proverbs 23:7 King James Version (Kjv)

Think (thought), belief, all start in the subconscious (heart?) and become our physical reality. Take note, it does not state that we control 100% of our destiny. Because I am so indoctrinated to the 'law of attraction', I think I somehow brought about every calamity in my life. In 2008, when the recession went deep, I blamed myself, my own 'self-sabotaging thoughts', for my business tanking. That's quite a burden of guilt to carry. Sometimes, it rains on your parade. You are not so powerful that your own thoughts caused it. It rained on everyone's parade. Remember that.

The term 'subconscious' and 'unconscious' mind is used interchangeably. Both represent a hypothetical physical organ, which has no actual existence, but is quite real. The subconscious directs our body to breathe, our heart to beat, and all the other autonomic processes our body does. The unconscious mind can tap into universal energy, be it positive or negative. Some call this "Infinite Intelligence'. Carl Jung called it the 'collective unconscious'. Our sense of who we are, of self-esteem and self-importance, is omnipresent in the unconscious. Freud called this our 'Ego'. When you have a sixth sense or intuition, this is the unconscious mind at work.

Ego directs us to behave in certain ways based upon it's understanding of what is appropriate for us. This can be good when it directs you not to fart in church. It's good when, if you are in danger, it directs you to take cover. It's not so good when it creates a fight or flight impulse because it fears you are getting too big for your panties. It's devastating when it wants to keep you playing small. Then, it makes you do stupid things, like sabotage your career, financial security or love life. It's disastrous when your unconscious believes you don't deserve love and respect, and thus attracts people into your life that abuse you, thereby proving the unconscious was right.

In other words, the 'Law of Attraction' works, and it works perfectly. There is plenty of evidence that our lives are self-fulfilling prophesies, but little was known about 'how' or 'why' this happened. Being analytical and a natural born skeptic, I needed to understand this phenomenon. What I learned sounded more like something you'd read in the National Inquirer than in a scientific journal. I can't begin to understand the mechanics of sub-atomic atoms and morphogenetic fields any more than I grasp how a movie can come across a wire into my TV, but I assure you, there is science behind the 'Law of Attraction'. Here are just some highlights that I find amazing.

<u>The Link Between Spirit and Matter</u>

In ancient cultures, there was a mystical connectedness. All forms of matter were in flow with the universe. In early science, no distinction was made between spirit and matter, between animate and inanimate things. So, a rock and a frog were both seen as living. Ancient Indians and Chinese cultures also saw the unity in all things. Mind, spirit and matter are connected. Duality began when a distinction was made between spirit and matter. Matter was seen as merely passive, essentially dead building blocks. Throughout history science and philosophy merged and separated.

Classical physics, which emerged in the 17th century, viewed mind and matter as separate. Sir Isaac Newton claimed what was real was only what one could see. Modern physicists of the late 1800's and early 1900's once again recognized the connection between mind/spirit and body. Between forces that one could not see and matter that is observable.

In the early 1920's physicists from all over the world joined forces or consciousness and made contact with this strange and unexpected reality of the sub-atomic world. The science of Quantum Physics was born. It explains that everything is energy; everything and everyone has its own vibration. Even an inanimate table is composed of sub-atomic atoms that are vibrating. While a table has an almost undetectable vibration, humans have a much higher vibration.

Our Bodies Have A Profound Electrical Nature.

Any beginning course on anatomy covers this. Shuffle your feet across a carpet and then touch an item made of metal and feel the electrical shock. Sometimes you can see static electricity that is discharged from your fingertip. Electrical messages are constantly sent throughout your body to keep it informed of what is going on. When our brain is given a certain stimulus, through our ears, eyes or other senses, it gives off an electrical charge called a 'cortical evoked response'. These electrical responses travel throughout the brain to become what we see and hear; in other words, what we experience. If you touch a hot stove you will feel the pain instantly because it is electrically transmitted along the nerves to your brain. The pain travels at the speed of electricity and that is why you feel the pain so quickly. These responses can also be measured with an EEG. Electroencephalography (EEG) is the recording of electrical activity along the scalp produced by the firing of neurons within our brain.

Have you had an EKG? Electrocardiography (ECG or EKG) is the process of recording the electrical activity of the heart over a period of time using electrodes placed on a patient's body. These electrodes detect the tiny electrical changes on the skin that arise from the heart muscle depolarizing during each heartbeat. Sometimes our frequencies (electro-magnetic) even cause our electronics to malfunction. (watches, computers, even vehicles). Now this sounds real twilight zone but, again, it is scientific fact. Here's an example.

A woman picked up her husband, who had just had brain surgery, from the hospital and started on the 200-mile journey home. Her husband was in fragile condition and could not tolerate extremes of heat and cold. Half-way home, in an isolated area with temps over 100 degrees, her SUV started making strange noises and the air conditioner began to malfunction. The woman felt desperate and panicked. She began talking to the car, asking for its help to get them home safely. She blessed the molecules that were holding the car together. Incredibly, the AC came back on accompanied by odd vibratory noises. They made it all the way home into the driveway when the car completely broke down. The car was towed to a auto repair shop the next day. The mechanic who repaired the car, thousands of dollars later, said what happened seemed impossible. There was no way she could have driven with the mechanical problem the car had.

Synchronicity

Jung was the first to explain the phenomenon of synchronicity. Synchronicity is the experience of two or more events that are apparently causally unrelated occurring together in a meaningful manner. Some examples of synchronicity include:

The wardrobe department for The Wizard of Oz unknowingly purchased a coat for character Professor Marvel from a second-hand store, which was later verified to have originally been owned by L. Frank Baum, the author of the novel on which the film was based.

Fourteen years prior to the sinking of the Titanic, the writer Morgan Robertson wrote the novel Futility, the central event of which is the sinking by a collision with an iceberg of the transatlantic Titan, described in the novel as allegedly unsinkable. Some of the circumstances in the novel match the actual disaster to an uncanny degree, including the number of passengers, the insufficient number of lifeboats, the name and size of the ship, the exact site of the incident, and the speed of the ship at the time of the collision. The coincidences have been noticed and the novel republished in the year following the actual disaster under the name The Wreck of the Titan.

Jung wrote, after describing some examples, "When coincidences pile up in this way, one cannot help being impressed by them—for the greater the number of them in such a series, or the more unusual its character, the more improbable it becomes."

Brainwave Entrainment (Aka Brain Synchronization)

Fact: while working on the design of the pendulum clock in 1656, Dutch scientists Christian Huygens found that if he placed two unsynchronized clocks side-by-side on a wall they would slowly synchronize to each other. Entrainment is defined as a synchronization of two or more rhythmic cycles. The principles of entrainment are universal, appearing in chemistry, neurology, biology, pharmacology, medicine, astronomy, and more.

Have you noticed that when two or more women work in close proximity their menstrual cycles begin to synchronize? Yikes! Half the office in PMS at one time.

Water Reacts to Emotions

Still not convinced about the power of thought? Consider this. Japanese scientist Dr. Masaru Emoto, photographed freezing water at microscopic levels after exposing them to different emotions written on paper. His photographs show us that water responds to conscious intentions by producing beautiful crystal snowflakes when exposed to loving and caring thoughts, and turns into ugly, dirty masses when exposed to negative thoughts. Remember our body is made up of 65 -75% water.

<u>Molecules of Emotion:</u>

Dr. Candace Pert, PhD, Author of 'Molecules of Emotion: The Science Behind Mind-Body Medicine' proved that thoughts actually become molecules. For example, when your subconscious mind is given the imagery of biting into a lemon, even though it was just an image, your subconscious mind creates a real molecule, a molecular messenger caused you to salivate and prepare for digestion. The thought of a lemon was an imagined one but the thought became a molecule anyway. This is why visualization and affirmations can be very powerful. If you vividly imagine an event, it can seem quite real. No matter how many times I watch Jaws I still experience the same fight or flight syndrome. My conscious mind knows the shark is just a machine, I've even seen it at Universal Studio, but my subconscious believes the stimuli it is given. When we attempt something risky that we have not done before (pubic speaking, sky-diving, marriage) we develop fear- fear of looking foolish, failing, getting hurt (expectations). Fear paralyzes us. But what if you have jumped out of 100 planes, received 100 standing ovations, or had a successful, loving marriage, would you be scared then? Well, you may always get butterflies before a speech or jumping out of a plane, or falling in love again, but it won't stop you. That is why imagining you have already done it quells the fear. It is also mental rehearsal. Olympic Gold Medalists, great actors, even politicians and astronauts, use mental rehearsal as much as physical practice. You will learn how to use affirmations and visualizations in a powerful way to influence your 'expectations'.

As I understand it, in layman terms, our thought molecules, smaller than a speck of dust are carried on electrical vibrations that are floating in the stratosphere, just as Carl Jung had explained with his 'collective unconscious' theory. Accordingly, there would be thought molecules from terrorists and mass murderers and from visionaries such as Gandhi and Mother Teresa as well as geniuses and Nobel prize winners. Rupert Sheldrake, PhD is a researcher in the field of parapsychology. He called the phenomena 'the morphogenetic field'. And, guess what, we can tap into those thoughts and make them our own. And, we do, whether we do it deliberately or unconsciously. This can be great news or really bad news.

Have you ever felt a negative thought or feeling that just seemed to float in from nowhere? This can be a result of the stream of the collective unconscious, or morphogenetic field you may have accidentally tapped into. Maybe you are just in close proximity to someone who is mourning. You feel their vibration even though you may not even know the person or that they are grieving. You instinctively want to move away from that vibration. I can also remember trying to sell houses when I was personally facing financial ruin. I used the same strategies, the same words that I had used to sell $3 million in real state the previous year, but I could not develop rapport with the clients. Now I know that I was sending a vibration that was not filled with love and caring for them, but was on a negative vibration of fear and desperation.

Incredibly, our thought vibrations can, and do reach great distances. Experiments at prestigious universities prove that when a group of people pray for someone far away, there is measurable results. Unfortunately, two weeks ago Hurricane Harvey wiped out a big chunk of Texas. And, now Irma is on it's way to Florida and has already devastated the Dominican Republic. Horrendous death and destruction is sending strong vibrations to the 'collective unconscious'. I sure feel it, even when I try not to. So, I send all the victims vibes of love and peace.

Vibrating with Love and Joy

Wouldn't it be wonderful if the world could vibrate with love and joy? We can do our part to keep pleasant thoughts. In one experiment performed at Heart Math Institute in Boulder Creek, California they had the participant concentrate on being grateful. The vibrations from this attitude of gratitude extended 9 feet from the participant and literally gave people within that circle a feeling of gratitude. Imagine being drawn to a person for no particular reason other than it 'feels good' to be near them. You are 'attracted' to their energy. And, what drives our behavior, is feelings.

Why you want what you want

What are we really looking for when we binge on chocolate cake or Smirnoff? It's not just the way it tastes. It is how it makes us feel, (before the eater's remorse sets in.). What are we getting from owning a Ferrari or being wildly successful? It makes us feel good. Why do we shop when we are blue? Why do we crave nicotine? All the above create a chemical change in the brain that makes us feel good. We crave, and get addicted, to having the high that our sin of choice gives us. Those damn thought molecules create very vivid mind pictures of moist chocolate cake glistening with fudge frosting. Oh, so hard to resist. Damn, now I want one.

Everything we do in life comes from our need to avoid pain and our desire to gain pleasure – both are biologically driven and constitute the controlling force in our lives. We will do far more to avoid pain than we will to gain pleasure. That could be the pain of letting something go. When you think about losing 100 pounds, you imagine the pain of dieting will be greater than the pleasure of being slender. But, when the doctor says you have 6 months to live if you don't lose 100 pounds, the pleasure of living outweighs the French fries. That's just the way our brains are programed. You've experienced it yourself. Maybe, you are in an abusive relationship but the fear of being alone (pain) is stronger than the pain of the abuse.

Thoughts create strong emotions and we feel those emotions in our body. We saw this earlier with love and gratitude. Now, think about a situation which really pissed you off. Really focus on it. (My 6-hour tech support experience does it for me). Where do you feel it in your body? Now, think about something you feel guilty about. Remember the details as vividly as you can. Notice how your body feels. For me, guilt starts with a constriction in my chest, (this must be where 'heart ache' comes from). Then, the constriction and tightness moves up to my head and I can feel tears welling up behind my eyes. My shoulders slump and I want to hide in shame. Definitely, not a place I want to stay very long.

Take a deep breath and shake off that negative emotion. Now, think about a very pleasant memory, perhaps your last vacation. Choose one day or one incident when you were particularly happy. For instance, you might imagine being on the Pirates of the Caribbean ride at Disneyland. Feel what it was like to be there, in the happiest place in the world. Imagine the sounds of crickets chirping and water rushing, feel the humidity in the air, and see the wonderful pirates teetering on barrels of rum. Where do you feel that in your body? I notice my chin goes up and I smile. My chest feels loose and expansive. I am breathing deeper.

Understand that others can feel your stress in their body. I'll bet you've felt sad just being in the presence of someone who is depressed. You may not even consciously realize they are despondent, yet you can't wait to get away.

Let's look at some of the positive and negative thoughts that create emotions:

POSITVE/EXPANSIVE	NEGATIVE/CONSTRICTED
Joy	Boredom
Love	Pessimism

Appreciation	Frustration
Gratitude.	Irritation, rage
Faith	Impatience
Passion	overwhelm
Enthusiasm, eagerness	disappointment
Positive expectations/beliefs	Negativity
Optimism	Pessimism
Hopefulness	Hopelessness, Powerlessness
Contentment	Worry/fear
Happiness	Blame, anger, resentment
Serenity	Hatred, jealousy, envy
Confidence	Insecurity
Admiration	Guilt
Pride	Unworthiness
Awe	Grief, depression, despair,

You can almost feel the shift in your body from just reading the words. We can choose to have thoughts, and thus the corresponding emotions, from the left column or from the right- usually. I know people who are depressed because the body is not producing serotonin and that chemical imbalance will cause them to feel sad no matter what. Certainly, if you are chronically feeling low, if your thoughts continually go to the dark side, seek medical help. However, for most of us, our gloom is a matter of our thoughts, not a chemical imbalance. Strong negative emotions can make you sick, even kill you. Guard your thoughts. My friend belongs to a group called 'Laugh Therapy'. They get together and simply laugh. Laughter is so contagious even the gloomiest participant feels the joy and starts laughing right along. Of course, the opposite is doubly true.

> "Anger is an acid that can do more harm to the vessel in which it is stored than to anything on which it is poured." Mark Twain

Socrates spoke of how you can hurt your enemy physically, and ruin him financially, even kill him, but that doesn't hurt his soul. The anger hurts your soul and ruins your enjoyable life. Anger eats away at your very core. It raises your blood pressure, disturbs sleep and digestion, and does other physical damage to your body. My friend Faye had a very traumatic event when she was about 60. Her brother beat her up and even broke her arm. She repeated the story over and over and held on vehemently to her rage and hatred. I swear, I watched her age 10 years in 4. Imagine living with that poisonous attitude. It did no harm to the brother, only Faye.

> "Most people are about as happy as they make up
> their minds to be." Will Rogers

'What is important to us is that we can choose to be happy. We can tap into the morphogenetic field, or collective unconscious, and connect with other like-minded thought molecules. If a butterfly flapping its wings in south America, can affect the weather patterns of the world, imagine what the vibrational frequency of a group of people can do. This is why we must choose our company carefully. There are some very effective ways to reach the subconscious and reprogram it.

TRANSFORMATION EXPLORATION 4: CONTROL YOUR STATE

Step One: Trigger the Power of Love

Sit comfortably and begin breathing evenly and fully. Now think about something that you love, something that you are not currently worried about. My Chi-Pom (Chihuahua- Pomeranian) is a happy thought, or Christmas morning when I was a kid. Okay, got a trigger? Now, be there and remember the scene with clarity. Hear the sounds of music, laughter, or the brook bubbling by. Is there an aroma? The pine scent from the Christmas tree. Concentrate on your trigger until you can feel it in your body. Now, take note of how you feel emotionally and physically. That is the state of love that you want to live in.

Step Two: Trigger worry

Put the love state aside for a moment and pick a worry trigger. Usually, it's easy to think of all the bad stuff. It's easy to recount every negative consequence, real or imagined. Allow the negative thought to invade your body and thus, your emotional state. Now check in with your body. How does it feel? Where do you feel it? Do you feel empowered, capable of handling whatever comes up? Imagine the vibration you are sending out. I was at an NLP training weekend just after Roy died and Tiffany cut me out of her life. I had a smile on my face, but I was crying on the inside. What do you think my colleagues saw? They saw the smile, but, they felt the grief. I felt like I was a Leper. People wanted to get away from me as fast as they could. You cannot hide your state.

Step Three: Trigger LOVE again.

I'm not going to leave you there. So, go back to the love memory or trigger. Feel the love and let it fill you with joy. Now, think about something for which you are grateful. Really, really feel the gratitude. Now add that emotion to the love. Stack another happy thought and let your entire body, mind and soul go into the state. You can evoke this feeling any time you want. How about before a sales appointment? Or, a blind date. You'll be irresistible!

SUMMARY:

Be careful what you think about

In the exercise above, you consciously decided to change your thoughts and experienced how your thoughts, even a word, can generate a feeling in your body. When we changed the thought, it changed our posture, our attitude, even our breathing. It's that simple! People think they can't help what they think. They can't help being depressed or negative. You see, you absolutely can 'help it'. We all have much more control over our brains than we realize. You just need the right tools. The next time you start thinking about something that makes you feel blue, or angry, or any emotion you don't want, just say, "STOP!" Your mind will fill in the rest, "STOP thinking about that!" Then, simply decide to think about something pleasant. It really is that simple. Have you ever had an 'ear-bug'? You know, a song that is playing in your mind until you think you're going crazy? Just say, "STOP!" You won't even be able to remember the tune.

Thoughts effect moods. Moods reflect in our actions. Actions determine our outcomes. Thought: I don't deserve love. Mood: depressed, unworthy. Actions: Push love away. Outcome: You don't get love.

HOW IT TRANSLATES PHYSICALLY

Reticular Activator System

How can our thoughts activate our behaviors? Medical researchers now know the physical mechanics of how we create our self-fulfilling prophecies. What determines our choices at any given moment? Depending on research you believe, in a typical day, we are bombarded with 2 Billion bits of sensory stimuli per second. Imagine if we had to consciously think about everything that is going on in our body: hair going down our neck after a haircut, clicking sound of the keyboard, hum of the fan, feeling of air on our skin, feel of our feet on the floor, our heartbeat, breathing, sirens, or the ticking of the clock. To be aware of all these stimuli would be mental bedlam. In fact, it would be impossible. We can only process about 2000 bits of information per second. Our RAS (Reticular Activating System) which is part of the brain stem, provides the filter to determine what 2000 bits of information we pay attention to. The RAS acts as a gate keeper preventing sensory overload. All the other bits are still there, but you literally don't know it, because the RAS doesn't let them in. so, you don't actually perceive reality, unless your RAS lets you. Our brains process information by: deleting, distorting and generalizing.

Only two categories of information are allowed in;

1. Information that is valuable for you to have right now.

If the stimuli fits the personality idea of what should be admitted, you will experience them. So, if there is stimuli that meets our expectations and belief in what is important, we are likely to see or hear it. If it doesn't meet our belief, we tend to not let the stimuli in. If you believe all men are louses, you will see only the men in the nightclub that meet that criteria. If you believe rich people are greedy or unscrupulous, you will find proof of that. Imagine you are in the airport terminal waiting for your flight. It's very noisy, people are talking, announcements are coming over the speaker system, and perhaps you're talking to your traveling companion. You aren't picking out any details about other conversations, or announcements, until you hear your name over the loud speaker. You immediately focus your attention on that announcement, although you didn't hear a word of what went before. That's your RAS at work – it has an instruction that says, 'Pay attention if you hear my name.'

Therefore, marketing language is so important. It's language that the RAS will pick up, and let in. And you'll get business. Your belief system is also controlled by the RAS. What makes your belief system so important is that your RAS is programmed, not by your conscious mind, but by your subconscious mind. So, any old messages, disempowering beliefs, and limiting thoughts that have gotten into your subconscious are still there, controlling your RAS, and your perception of reality, and, of what is possible. Eventually, over time, information from your conscious mind will seep in- eventually with work, over months or years. But to get to the subconscious more quickly, we need cutting-edge belief change systems.

Your beliefs DO affect what you perceive, and what's possible for you – and that affects your success in ALL that you do. Since the RAS acts as our 'executive secretary', our 'gatekeeper', we need to know what instructions it has been given, so that we know what's coming into our perception. Our RAS programming exists in our subconscious, not our conscious mind. But what's in the subconscious that controls the RAS?

The problem comes when the RAS contains erroneous or incomplete data. For example, if I have a fear of public speaking, my model of information about public speaking includes the idea that I am in terrible danger when I'm speaking. (Of course, this is just my subconscious mind, but in a battle between the conscious and the subconscious, the subconscious wins every time.) And when part of our model of information includes a message of danger, we are usually unable to accurately perceive the REST of the model. For example, with public speaking, I can't see that people might be enjoying my speaking, I can't rationally know that I'm not in physical danger, because my entire being is screaming 'DANGER!' This is an example of erroneous data in my RAS. And it's NOT in the conscious mind, as anyone with a fear of public speaking knows.

What does this mean for us in our daily business or life routine? Whenever we are irritated, angry, afraid, sad, upset, or any other negative emotion, there is some element in our model of information that's creating those negative emotions. Then, the negative emotions will, in turn, cause us to act in ways that create additional situations that feed our erroneous programming even more. With new beliefs, everything changes. Opportunities appear that just weren't present before. Negative emotions vanish, and it becomes far easier for us to achieve and accomplish in our lives. Our relationships with others (and with ourselves!) improve, our relationship with our business, our finances, our lives all shift.

You become happier, both in pursuing your measures of success and in receiving them. While happiness is great, this isn't just about feeling good. This is about being able to do things that you've never done before. This is about achievement, and success

2. Treat or danger. You can be totally engaged in a project, but the slightest smell of gas will alert you to danger. We can also perceive danger where it doesn't exist such as my fear of wealth. The RAS does not do a good job of distinguishing between real and perceived danger.

The Vagus Nerve (AKA cranial nerve X)

The VN (Vagus Nerve) is the only nerve that starts in the brainstem within the medulla oblongata & extends through the juggler foramen down below the head, to the back, chest and abdomen. It also plays a role in directing our destiny. For our bodies to perform trillions of functions simultaneously, our cells must communicate faster than thoughts form, faster than the speed of light, more than 186,000 miles per second.

The VN relays sensory information about the state of the body's organs to the central nervous system, Basically, the Vagus Nerve takes care of all the automatic actions in the body. Get cold and the VN tells the body to start shaking to warm up. It is like a two-way radio between our thoughts and our bodily reactions. Touch a hot stove and our VN instantly pulls the hand away. Think fear and our body goes into fight or flight. Of course, the problem is that, our fears are not always real, right? So, all our imaginary fears that hold us back have a physical result.

SUMMARY:

I hope this little section gave you more insight into the forces that drive your behavior, and thus your circumstances. You will see many examples of the RAS in action throughout this book and in everyday life.

DECODE HOW YOUR BRAIN WORKS

"The greatest discovery of my generation is that man can alter his life by altering his attitudes of mind." William James

ALTER YOUR LIFE BY CHANGING YOUR THROUGHTS

William James was one of the leading thinkers and philosophers of the late nineteenth century and is referred to as the "Father of American psychology". He had a medical degree, but never practiced. He was a brilliant intellect about metaphysics, science and religion. He spent his life investigating the unexplained laws of nature and the powers latent in man. (Meaning mankind, I presume. Women were never mentioned.) What James and others of his generation discovered, 'that men can change their lives by changing their thoughts', had been understood by only a few enlightened souls prior to the 19th century. The discovery should've changed the world. However, apparently, the world wasn't ready. Also, the tools that could make it happen, had yet to be developed. Just 'how to' change your thoughts remained a mystery.

The success or personal development books advised us to visualize and affirm our goals and they would magically appear. That is simply not true. You can visualize your slender body 'til the cows come home and still be fat. You can affirm over and over, "I am fabulously wealthy.", and still be broke. That is what frustrated me for years. I didn't know that those tools, while helpful, do little to impact the subconscious where our beliefs are held.

I'm not saying that visualizations and affirmations are not valuable tools for change. I know they are and, I'll teach you how impressive the results can be if you use 'your mind's eye' (visualization) and 'self-talk' (affirmations, declarations) in the right way. 'Who' you think you are, your self-image, is exactly a matter of the 'who' you see in your mind's eye. Not the 'who' you see in the mirror. 'Who' you think you are, is reinforced by the self-talk we engage in. I'm saying, just because you visualize and affirm that you are a terrorist, doesn't make you one. Nor, does pretending to be a famous ballerina make it true. I pretended to be rich and successful. I vividly imagined it. I proclaimed it. But what happened? I couldn't sustain it because I had not addressed my unconscious fears and beliefs. And, none of the books told me how to do that. Even the "Secret" falls short. It does a great job of convincing us that we are what we think, but does not give us real tools for changing what we think.

You see, visualizations and affirmations barely impact the unconscious where our programs are stored. Sure, the billionaires and great people that Napoleon Hill researched, used affirmations and practiced seeing their positive outcomes, but, is that what made them great? I think, they already had an unconscious belief in themselves. Maybe, they were using affirmations and visualization to reinforce what they believed to be true. In other words, the affirmations and visualizations were congruent with their self-concept.

MASLOW'S HIERARCHY OF HUMAN NEEDS

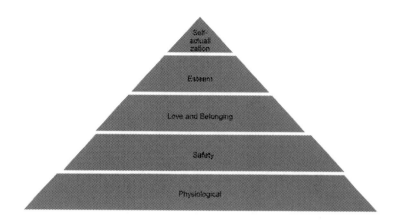

Abraham Maslow was a psychologist, who in 1950, created this pyramid of human needs and explained it in his book 'Motivation and Personality'. He explains that we all, every single one of us, most satisfy certain needs before we can move up to higher needs. Looking at the bottom of the pyramid, you see the very basic physiological needs: Water, breath, sleep, food. If you were 100 feet under water and your scuba tank ran out oxygen, I promise, you won't be worrying about your foreclosure notice. If you were standing on your roof in Katrina, waiting to be rescued, you wouldn't be fretting about your marital problems. You are focused on surviving, no more. When you are out of immediate danger, say the helicopter has picked you up, the next thing you will be thinking about is safety.

Now, you want to ensure you will reach high ground and have water and food. You would not be considering your lofty goals or your next vacation. You have gone from survival to security. Before you can leave this level you have to take care of situations that jeopardize your families wellbeing. Security can mean stable employment, a safe environment, urgent medical care. Does it make sense to you that you will not be concerned with the higher need self-actualizing at this point? When you have safety and security met then you can move to Love and Belonging.

On this level you need to be accepted and approved of by your tribe so you belong. Mankind is not autonomous; indeed, we could not stay mentally healthy if we were deprived of human companionship for an extended period. We need love. We need to belong. Some people spend a lot of time on this level. They are always trying to impress people with how rich and successful they are so they would be admired and loved. But, most of us simply conform to our peers. This is a real stumbling block if you want to be more and have more, than the pack. To rise to the next level, 'Esteem', you must not be afraid of rejection. That is a biggie for most people. Fear that our friends and family will abandon us if we are not like them, is fatal to success.

'Esteem' includes self-esteem, confidence, achievement, respect of others and by others. On this level we want to excel and be better than average. We've let go of the fear of abandonment. We want recognition. We collect merit badges; trophies, plaques, and awards. And we feel proud of our achievements. We want to stand above the crowd, so to speak. This is a good thing and if you don't think so, you're in trouble.

At the top of pyramid is 'Self-Actualization'. When you reach this peak, you don't care what others think, you achieve for your own joy, just to see how much more you can do. Richard Branson, one of the world's richest men, doesn't work for money. He could never spend what he has in his lifetime. (Well, maybe he could if he buys another island or airline.) He doesn't work for ego gratification. He just loves to see what else he can do that, maybe, he didn't know if he could do. What a wonderful place to strive for.

20TH CENTURY CHANGE MASTERS

In the second half of the 20th century methods for helping people transform, at an unconscious level, were being created. Virginia Satir, acclaimed author and family therapist, was known to get phenomenal results in her family therapy practice. She created the Virginia Satir Change Process Model, a method that exacted rapid and impressive change in her patients. Milton Erickson was an American psychiatrist and psychologist who was renowned for the results he achieved with his patients using medical hypnosis to heal patients physically and psychologically. Fritz Perl, a German born psychiatrist and psychoanalyst, was also acclaimed for his ability to create phenomenal change in his patients through a unique form of psychotherapy which he named 'Gestalt therapy'.

EMOTIONAL FREEDOM TECHNIQUE (EFT)

I was looking for something to entertain myself while on my exercise bike and I came across my old EFT course. I had forgotten how mindboggling this technique is. If you saw someone doing it without knowing what is, you would have them committed. EFT is based upon the discovery that imbalances in the body's energy system have profound effects on one's personal psychology. Correcting these imbalances, which is done by tapping on certain body locations, often leads to rapid transformations. By rapid, I mean, most of the problems vanish in minutes! I watched the trainer help some veterans with PTSD (post-traumatic stress disorder) that had disabled them for years. Then he helped a man with a horrendous fear of water, one with a fear of heights, and a lady who had been sexually abused by her brother as a child. It was interesting to see that phobias, and even addictions, could be annihilated with just one session.

EFT is often described as 'a needle-free version of acupuncture' because it clears the energy blockages along the body's meridian pathways and proposes that most, if not all, illnesses are caused by unresolved emotional issues. This applies to weight problems, fear of success and even, migraine headaches.

It is an unbelievably simple and easy procedure that anyone can perform on themselves.

I highly recommend you consider EFT. Practitioners who are trained in EFT are usually trained in more than one mode of transformational work. They may be licensed family therapists or NLP Practitioners, coaches or other professionals. But honestly, you can do it yourself. Just buy a course online.

NLP (NEURO-LINGUISTIC PROGRAMMING) MASTERY OR WOO-WOO?

In the 1970s two young men at UC Santa Cruz. Richard Bandler, a graduate psychology student, and John Grinder an assistant professor of linguistics were challenged by their mutual mentor, Gregory Bateson, to go and research what it takes to be excellent at something. They began their quest by studying the three change masters above. They studied everything about these great practitioners, the words they used, the tone of voice, and body language; even their attitudes and beliefs. From this, they developed a model of a successful change master. They then created a system of tools, techniques and processes which they taught to others. When they endowed the person with the same attributes, at a subconscious level, the recipient could get similar results to these exceptional models. They named the technique Neuro-Linguistic Programming (NLP for short). Neuro-for the physical or neurological involvement. The mental pathways of our five senses by which we see, hear, feel, taste, small. Linguistic- refers to our ability to use language and how specific words and phrases mirror our mental worlds. Linguistic also refers 'silent language' of postures, gestures, and habits that reveal our thinking styles, beliefs and more. Programming, because our thoughts, feelings and actions are simply habitual programs that can be changed by upgrading our mental software.

In the four decades since this phenomenal discovery, NLP practitioners have further developed hundreds of models for every area of life. There is a model for creativity from the study of Walt Disney. There is a model for how to be a great reader or speller. NLP has applications that have been applied to psychotherapy, medicine-therefore physical illness, law, education, physical performance-sports in other words, and even love and happiness. Some of the most important areas of change through NLP are self-esteem, self-worth, and self-confidence. Imagine being able to change your self-esteem or remove some limitation in a brief session as opposed to years of traditional therapy. While traditional clinical psychology is primarily concerned with describing difficulties, categorizing them, and searching for historical cause, NLP is interested in *how* our thoughts, actions and feelings work together right now to produce our experience.

Anthony Robbins, the Father of Life Coaching, is our most illustrious practitioner. I can watch him for hours as he changes lives in 15 minutes.

Think of NLP exercises as training your brain. It would be great if an NLP coach could guide you through the processes, but you can do the ones in this book by yourself. I began studying NLP in 2007 for three primary reasons.

1. I couldn't bring myself out of the grieving for my dear friend and ex-husband, Roy and our 30-year-old daughter, Tiffany For after Roy had that fatal heart attack, my

      beautiful Tiffany disowned me. I've only seen her and my granddaughter about 6 times in 11 years.

2. After twelve years of rapid success in our Design & Build Remodeling Firm, our business was faltering. I feared it might be my old self-sabotage returning. I had to get control. Looking back, I realize it was a combination of the 2007 recession, burn-out and grief.

3. I wanted to become a transformational speaker-trainer and I felt like my old teachings about the 'Law of Attraction' were obsolete. I assumed everyone already knew all that. I wanted the latest technology. Of course, the 'Law of Attraction' is even more popular than ever.

I definitely wasn't operating from my higher-self, so I enrolled. All three of my goals were achieved, and so much more. During my training to become a Master Practitioner, I witnessed and experienced unbelievable transformations. I can honestly say, some bordered on miracles. A lessor example was one lady from the East Bay who was so afraid of bridges, that rather than cross one, she would drive an extra 90 minutes around the south bay to get to our class in South San Francisco. When Tim Hallbum, (the awesome trainer and founder of NLP Institute of California) began working with Bev, the mere thought of a bridge made her cry uncontrollably. Within minutes Tim had finished a procedure on her and we thought no more about it until we saw Bev again at the next meeting. We were all curious about her results and when queried Bev boasted that she came across the bridge and the fear was completely gone.

One day, Tim asked for volunteers who had a physical issue. For the six years since I had injured my right shoulder, I had been gradually losing the use of my arm. I had recently consulted with a new surgeon and she had informed me that I was permanently disabled and that my arm would begin to atrophy and just hang by my side. It was also painful and I couldn't raise it more than a few inches. In fact, the physical therapist had put my arm in a cast and a sling. When Tim invited me to the stage, I told him that there was nothing that could be done for my arm. After all, I have no tendons at all to move the arm and the doctor told me It was impossible to regain any use. Tim insisted. In literally three minutes I was raising my arm above my head. Everyone was astonished! I saw the surgeon a few weeks later and I asked her what the purpose of the appointment was. She answered that I was to receive electrical shock for the constant, debilitating pain. I said, 'What pain? I don't have pain.' She was stunned. Then she reminded me that I could not lift the arm. I raised my arm above my head and exclaimed, 'You mean I can't do this?' You should've seen the look on her face, it was priceless. I told her it was the result of NLP and she scoffed. Of course, it wasn't possible.

It's been ten years since Tim performed his magic on me and my arm has not atrophied and I am still able to us it, albeit not to the full extent I had before the accident, and it still hurts if I overuse it. But, by Jove, I get by pretty darned good. I cringe when I realize that, had Tim not changed that belief, which is exactly what it was, a 'belief' that my arm would atrophy, I would not even be able to do my hair today. Wow! I was blessed twice, first Mom manipulated my limp arm when I was a baby, then Tim. I had no clue that my mind could make my body transform. Actually, there is plenty of evidence of this. Dennis Waitley, psychologist to the first astronauts, and many Olympic athletes, specialized in psychosomatic medicine. He claims to have seen proof that 'mental obsessions have physical manifestations'. He believes in the prophecy:

> "You indeed become what you most imagine or fear;
> you bring to pass what you suspect; you become the
> person you expect to become".

NLP is referred to as the science of the mind and is often called the User's Manual for the Brain. NLP is a methodology that discovers how our brain interprets, sorts, and stores our experiences and emotional life on a fundamental level. Once interpreted, NLP processes directly impacts these thoughts and can literally change (reprogram) the beliefs at a subconscious level. When that happens, there is a miraculous transformation. NLP is based upon new principles of how the mind/brain works. These principles or assumptions are called NLP Presuppositions. If we could summarize all the NLP Presuppositions in one phrase, it would be: *People work perfectly.* Our thoughts, actions and feelings consistently produce specific results. We may be happy or unhappy with these results, but if we repeat the same thoughts, actions, and feelings, we'll get the same results. The process works perfectly. If we want to change our results, then we need to change the thoughts, actions, and feelings that produced that result. Once you have the tools to do that, life flows much more effortlessly. There are two fundamental principles and several pre-suppositions.

The Map is not the territory. Meaning, a map of California is not really California. If you burn the map you don't burn California. In the same respect, our beliefs are based on our own unique experiences and are not necessarily reality. It is not possible to know reality directly; we know it only through our senses. As information passes through our sensory organs and is processed by the brain, it gets distorted, deleted and generalized. The way the information is transformed is governed by our mental and emotional fibers, by our beliefs, and by our focus of attention (the RAS- reticular activating system). The RAS filters, based upon pre-programmed beliefs and are highly individual. What is stressful to one, is peaceful to another. What is funny to one, is boring to another. Each one of us can only respond to our map of reality, and these massive realities are widely different. It is silly to get upset at someone thinking or responding differently than yourself, because if you had their map of reality, you would think and respond the same way they do. It is not what happens to us that impacts who we are, but how we interpret or 'code' what happens to us. One child raised in the ghetto will decide based on their experience and messages they received, that they're only destiny is to become a prostitute or live a life of crime. While another reaches tremendous heights of success and becomes a philanthropist. You might call these interpretations, subconscious or unconscious beliefs or expectations.

<u>Energy flows where attention goes.</u> The exercise machine of the mind is attention; where ever you direct it the energy flows and the part under focus becomes stronger. If you focus on illness, you give power to it. If you focus on trouble, you give power to that. If you focus on how much you love, you give power to that. Have you ever observed, how, after you decided on a new Infiniti, you begin seeing them everywhere? This is why we should focus on gratitude every single night before we fall asleep. Keep a journal by your bed and make notes of just one or two things that you are grateful for that day. Look at it again and maybe even add one. "I am grateful for waking up to another glorious day!" It's amazing how your RAS will start seeing things to reinforce your attitude of gratitude.

Here is a list of NLP Presuppositions:

1. <u>Behind every behavior is a positive intention.</u> Yes, every single behavior. Even Hitler's. It is important to understand that the positive intent is (often) for the person himself, not for other people. Similarly, every one of your behaviors has a positive intent for some part of you. Maybe not for the whole of you, but for the part doing the behavior. Smoking is clearly not healthy overall, yet it often has many positive intents such as relaxation, social acceptance or mental escape.

2. <u>People always make the best choice they can at the time.</u> People live in their maps of reality, and always choose

the best option they can see. It might not be your or our best options, but for them it seems the best. If someone is making a poor choice, just keep in mind that they either don't know what else they can do or don't understand that a better option exists. Until we become enlightened, our minds have different parts or roles that were activated at different times, and depending on which part is active at the moment, people have different sets of choices available to them at different times. The part that's running the show at the moment always makes the best choice for itself, even if it's unhealthy for the rest of you. So, stop beating yourself up for all the dumb things you've done.

3. <u>Choice is better than no choice.</u> Remember, we always make the best choice we can at the time. As we gain more self-awareness we can add more choices, thus increasing the quality of our decisions. Get off the fence, do something.

4. <u>Anyone can do anything given the right strategy.</u> This belief is highly useful and empowering. This belief is essential to manifest your dreams. Think of it this way-can you fly an airplane? Likely not. Yet, with precise step-by-step instructions, you can become a pilot, and it's easier than you think. The key is small-chunk, step-by-step instruction, e.g. pull this lever, look at that dial, push the blue button. When you reduce anything that looks complicated, be it high-yield investing, enlightenment or writing a best-selling book, into small enough steps that anyone can follow, anyone can do it.

5. <u>There is no such thing as failure, only feedback.</u> I love this one! Supposedly, Edison tried 9,999 ways to make a light bulb. When his colleague asked him how he able to deal with all the failure, Edison replied, "I haven't failed. I just found 9,999 ways it won't work." What an inspiring way to look at it. In fact, if you want to succeed you better have this belief. If not, you will feel like a failure and that produces

a state-of-mind that results in depression and negativity, in which case, you are doomed to failure.

6. <u>The meaning of the communication is the response you get.</u> Whenever you are communicating with others it is your job to get your point across. If they don't get it you didn't say it the right way *for them*. If they blow you off, you didn't create enough rapport. If they get angry and defensive, you didn't say it in a way that defuses their defenses. Remember, they are interpreting what you say from their own map. My daughter, Heidi, is a confident, high level, manager at the Department of Justice. One day I was trying to do something on my computer and she was kibitzing me. Obviously, she didn't realize how much I knew about word processing and was trying to help. I teased her, "Oh, I see, you are a micro-manager." She exploded! "How could you say such an insulting thing to me?" she yelled. She even cried. I was blown away. What in the world had I said? Little did I know that a few years' prior, Heidi had been taken to task by a superior for 'micro-managing'. She thought she had corrected it. I'm sure she had. My innocent teasing had ignited a fury of emotions.

7. <u>The words we use are not the person.</u> In other words, you can say despicable things and not be a despicable person.

8. <u>What you resist, will persist.</u> Action comes out of acceptance, not resistance.

9. <u>There are no un-resourceful people, only un-resourceful states.</u> When a person is angry or afraid, the strong emotion blocks their ability to find solutions.

10. <u>A person's behavior is not who they are.</u> Children sometimes act up. They can do bad things. That doesn't mean they are inherently bad. If a teenager becomes promiscuous, it doesn't mean she is a slut (as my mother thought). The behavior is caused by a screwed-up map. Remember, the behavior has a positive intent. Maybe to feel loved.

11. <u>Communication is redundant.</u> You are always communicating, in all three major representational systems. If you detest something it shows in your facial expression (body language), words you say and how you say them, and in in the actions you take.

12. <u>Requisite variety.</u> The element in a system with the most flexibility will be the controlling element.

13. <u>People work perfectly.</u> No one is wrong or broken; it's simply a matter of finding out how they function now, so that you can effectively change that to something more useful or desirable. People don't need to be "fixed".

14. <u>Every behavior is useful in some contexts.</u> While yelling and screaming at your child may make you a bad mother, the behavior is useful if they are about to run into the street.

NLP is an effective and rapid form of psychological therapy capable of addressing the full range of problems which psychologists encounter. For instance, depression, behavior disorders, psychosomatic illnesses, learning disorders, allergies, phobia and much more. It has already changed the lives of millions of people around the world and is changing our understanding of psychology. It is used in education, sports, health, and even spirituality with incredible results. With NLP things that were once thought impossible are becoming commonplace, and being systematically achieved by people just like you and me. NLP is taught at universities in Europe. Traditional forms of therapy such as Gestalt can take years to facilitate change, NLP can accomplish the same results in one or two sessions. Many traditional therapists are now incorporating it in their practices. NLP has made break throughs in PTSD. It has been used successfully to cure claustrophobia in patients who could not endure MRIs. Here's some of what has been said about NLP:

"Neuro-Linguistic-Programming has untapped potential for treating individual problems.

It's metamorphosed into an all-purpose self-improvement program and technology." Time Magazine

"NLP could be the most important synthesis of knowledge about human communication to emerge since the sixties." Science Digest

"NLP may be the most powerful vehicle for change in existence today."

Modern Day Psychology Magazine

ANCHORS AND TRIGGERS

Have you ever heard a song and had a strong feeling or emotion pass through you? Or smelled sweet potato pie baking in the oven and got a feeling of wellbeing? When you see a Christmas tree all lit up, do you feel happy? It could be that the aroma, sound or sight of something triggered an unconscious memory. Events in our lives are associated with emotions. The more impactful the event, the stronger the emotion.

In NLP (Neuro-linguistic Programming) we refer to this as 'anchoring'. An anchor is anything that creates an instant feeling. That is what happens in veterans who have PTSD. They hear the fireworks and it puts them in a state of terror because the sound takes them right back to a life-threatening situation. The sound (anchor) *triggered* the emotion. When I hear Anne Murray sing 'Could I Have This Dance for The Rest of My Life' (anchor) I feel loved, contented, and secure all at once. It was my wedding song with John. On the other hand, I heard Beethoven's 5th one day and I instantly felt distressed, almost ill. The feeling was so overwhelming I had to turn off the radio. I quickly remembered that I had listened to that tape while I was having my chemo treatments that made me sick as a dog. To this day, the smell of cut grass (anchor) triggers being a contented 5-year-old when Daddy mowed the lawn at a house we only lived in six months. For many years after the two cops slammed me to the ground, handcuffed me, and told me I was being arrested for attempted murder, every time I saw a cop (anchor), I went into a state of terror. Even now, almost 50 years later, when I watch Dateline and see an innocent person freed after 20 years in prison, I feel fear.

It's not a conscious thing, thus you can't control it with conscious thoughts. The anchor, cut grass, a sweet-potato-pie in the oven, a song, or any event creates the anchor. From then, any time you encounter the anchor, it triggers the emotion.

I highly recommend you find a Master Practitioner in your area and treat yourself to a session. Some even give a complimentary intro session. I got my training at NLPCA www.nlpca.com, which is in the San Francisco bay area and in Oregon. I highly recommend them.

TRANSFORMATION EXPLORATION 5: ANCHORS AWAY

1. List five or more anchors in your life and how they make you feel.
2. Describe an incident when you were sending out a negative vibration and how others reacted to you.
3. Clarify your understanding of your own spirituality.

SEEING IS BELIEVING

Some people say, "I'll believe it when I see it." This is absolutely true with our dreams and goals. If you can't see yourself, in your mind's eye (imagination), with the goal achieved, you won't believe it. And, we know, if you don't believe it, you won't get it. So, if you can't imagine yourself slender, or rich, or happily married, you're sunk.

Some people think they can't visualize. That could be because they are more dominant in one of the other five senses. We're all different. Maybe you've always been artistic. You love to draw, decorate and create things of beauty. If so, making mental pictures is natural for you. Maybe you love books and words. If so, you may hear with your minds ear instead. Maybe you are very intuitive and can feel emotions in a room. You are more kinesthetic. One sense may be dominant, but I think you will learn, that you do visualize. For instance, where is your car? A picture of your car in the driveway may flash in your mind's eye. What color is your mother's hair. Did her face flash in your imagination for a brief moment? The skill of visualization can be learned and improved upon.

I'm sure you've heard about visualization, but, do you understand how powerful it is? We all visualize to some extent. Fear is unintentionally seeing some future outcome go wrong. This is negative visualization and must be avoided. But, intentional visualization can help reinforce a goal or behavior or even, belief, that is congruent with your self-expectation. Athletes, even Olympic Champions, use the process. Business people and politicians, rock stars and astronauts, use it. It's nothing more than mental rehearsal.

Dr. Charles Garfield, former NASA researcher and current president of the Performance-Science Institute in Berkeley, California, explained the mind-power phenomenon using a startling experiment conducted by Soviet sports scientists back in 1980. The study participants were world-class athletes at their physical peak. Just prior to their entrance into the 1980 Olympics in Lake Placid, New York, these athletes were divided into four test groups.

- Group 1, who went through 100% physical training.
- Group 2, who went through 75% physical training and 25% mental training.
- Group 3, who went through 50% physical training and 50% mental training.
- Group 4, who went through 25% physical training and 75% mental training.

Can you see where this is going? Which group do you think saw the greatest increases in performance?

The most successful group at that year's Olympics was Group 4, who concentrated most of their training on cognitive aspects. That's not what the researchers expected – and it's probably not what you expected, was it? Group 4 saw significantly greater improvement than Group 3... Group 3 showed more improvement than Group 2, and Group 2 showed more improvement than Group 1. The athletes who practiced mental rehearsal showed the most improvement. With mental power, the athletes were able to improve their physical power. Imagine what you will experience with your individual goals when you put creative visualization into action in your life!

To better understand the processes, let's start with a simple exercise. Have you ever ridden on a roller coaster or some other amusement park ride? Take a moment and recall a specific ride. Then imagine that you are sitting on a bench some distance away, watching yourself on the ride. Notice how you feel in your body. Now, step into your seat on the ride, so that you can feel your hands on the cool, metal guardrail in front of you. Feel the pull as the train chugs up, up, up, to the highest peak. Hear the clicking or the wheels. Look down at the ground and see the people, and the scenery below. Finally, you crest the top and start speeding down, down, down. Feel the force of the wind pushing you back. Hear the screams. Notice how you feel as you experience being on the ride. This is very different than watching yourself on the ride from a distance.

These two very different perspectives have different mental structures. Being on the ride is engaging and exciting. NLP calls this 'associated'. Watching the ride is detached and unemotional. This is called 'disassociated'. You'll discover that every experience we have has these and many other common structures. If you want to get excited about something, you'll need to get involved, physically and mentally, by stepping into the experience, associating into it. You can learn how to do this at will. On the other hand, all of us also have experiences in our lives when some objectivity, some men[tal] distance, would be calming and very helpful. By stepping ou[t] these experiences, and out of the intense feelings they stir up, w[e] easily become more resourceful and creative in dealing wit[h] Being able to deliberately use these mental structures of e[x] is an incredible ability.

Now, try this 'thought experiment'. Begin with a clea[r]... by scanning your body for any tension and consci[...] think of a pleasant experience, some specific eve[...] really happy. Get 'associated'. Really be in your [...] it. Now, in your mind's eye,

- Make it vivid. Make the picture in... color, with every detail. What a[re]... with you? What does the roo[...] window? Is the client acros[s]... in and hanging on your... admiration in her eyes....
- Intensity. You must fe[...] mind. Feel yourself... pen in your hand... your breathing...

[overlapping diagonal text fragments] ...this ...Now, you were you imagine ...mind vivid, in living wearing? Who is there like? Can you see out a you? Imagine her leaning word. See the respect and with every cell of your body and ...dently asking for the order. Feel the ...he hard, cold surface of the desk. Feel ...he temperature in the room. Feel the soft silk of your blouse, the fabric of your skirt. Especially, feel the excitement of the sale. "YES! I aced this sale." (We'll talk about affirmations later.).

- Move it closer. Allow the event to move closer to you.
- Make it larger and brighter and more colorful.
- Notice your feelings again. Have they changed, perhaps gotten stronger?
- Now, take the same experience and move it farther away from you in your mind's eye, getting smaller, dimmer. Keep moving it out until it is the size of a postage stamp. Now, note your feelings. Has the emotion diminished? Finally, allow the experience to return to normal.

Your concentration should be focused mostly on what you feel. Imagine how it will feel to be slender or to get a standing ovation. [Wh]at motivates us is always how 'it' will make us feel. We want [financ]ial security because it will make us feel 'peace'. We want love [pl]us feel secure or valued. Always concentrate of how it feels.

think . imagine that it could be that simple to change how you
the way about a situation? Most people say, "Well I can't help
to rememb or feel". But now you know, you can. If you want
and make it ny time, simply move it closer in your mind's eye
memory, move 1 We call this changing modality. If it is a sad
nd fade it.

If you want to find lo
tall, dark, handsome gir creative visualization. Not to see some
walking on the beach han a white horse. Focus on the feeling of
with that person. In this w hand, enjoying meals, and laughing
coincides with your desires. ou'll attract the love who truly

TRANSFORMATIONAL EXPLORATION 6: EXPECTATION

In order to visualize correctly, you need to learn how your unique brain works- how you represent something in your mind's eye that you expect to have, or do, verses how you represent something you don't expect to have happen.

Using space anchors intensifies the results. However, you can also just use your imagination.

1. First create your Anchors
2. Using an 8 ½ x11 sheet of paper, create two anchors and place them on the floor.

EXPECTED	UN-EXPECTED

3. Step onto EXPECTED anchor.
   Think of something that you fully and without reservation expect to happen. *Going to bed tonight? Driving to the office tomorrow morning?*
4. Go inside and notice how it is. Notice the quality of the internal pictures (color, brightness, clarity, number of pictures, is it framed or panoramic). Notice the sounds and voices (tonal qualities, volume, pitch), and your feelings (tactile senses, sense of motion, action sense).
5. Write these qualities down to keep track of them.
   Get 3 examples and internalize the way you feel, what you see, etc.
6. Step onto the UN-EXPECTED anchor
   Use the same process to code something that you'd like to have happen but *don't* expect to manifest. *Win the lottery. Workout at gym.*

7. Notice the difference.
8. Write it down

TRANSFORMATION EXPLORATION 7: FUTURE PACE

1. Replace the un-expected anchor with a new spatial anchor for the goal. Then, stepping onto the expectation anchor, think about all the qualities of 'expectation'.

| EXPECTATION | ➡ | Be Fit and Trim |

2. Now, step onto the goal anchor taking those qualities with you. Holding the expectation thoughts, code the new goal in the same way.
3. Start future pacing. Imagine you are 1, 5, 10 years into your future. Exactly, what does it look and *feel* like to have attained your goal?

So, now you are an expert visualizer. After you find your values, passion and purpose, and set goals, you'll use visualization to reinforce them.

SUMMARY:

You can be your own NLP Practitioner and change almost anything about yourself. You can also use the tools you are learning to help others change. Of course, it is better to be coached through this by a professional, but I guarantee you will also benefit by doing it alone.

KEY #4

GET TO KNOW YOURSELF

"What you exhibit outwardly, you are inwardly. You are the product of your own thought. What you believe yourself to be, you are." —Claude Bristol, 'The Magic of Believing'

PART I: BELIEFS

How well do you really know yourself? Do you understand why you have made some of the decisions in life that have brought you grief? In this section, you will discover answers to these questions. As you write your life story, which you will do soon, you may be astonished to learn how you interpreted events in your life and thus the resulting behaviors and circumstances. But, let's start uncovering some of your beliefs that may or may not, be serving you well. Some may sound like facts, but look further, they could be beliefs.

Take this little quiz

True	False	I can't be rich because I am a good person
True	False	I don't have what it takes to succeed
True	False	I don't deserve to have a good life.
True	False	I'll never be rich, that's for other people
True	False	Rich people are better than me
True	False	I'm too fat for men to be attracted to me
True	False	I was molested as a child; therefore, I am nasty and unlovable
True	False	I am ashamed to want to get rich.
True	False	Rich people are arrogant snobs and I am nice so I can't be rich
True	False	You have to work hard to be successful and sacrifice time with your family
True	False	I was told "My dreams of were unrealistic", so why try?
True	False	I'm not lovable (worthy)
True	False	If I have money people will try to take it
True	False	If you get to know me, you won't like me.
True	False	Money doesn't buy happiness.

In and of themselves, the above statements don't mean much. However, I'll bet one or two gave you a small jolt. Maybe even an 'Ah-ha!' Circle the ones that you felt the most energy around. You can delve into these later. In a chapter 9, there are several belief change processes. But, for now, we aren't through finding the beliefs.

What we believe

As I said, if you want to know what your unconscious expectations or *beliefs* are, just look around you. If you say you have good self-esteem but live with an abuser, your actions speak louder than your words. If you say you want to be slender but keep eating 3000 calories a day, there is a part of you that does not want to be slender. Claude Bristol was not referring to our conscious thought, but rather, the unconscious beliefs that show up in our life circumstances.

Belief is described as: a psychological state in which an individual holds a proposition or premise to be true; despite a lack of evidence and often, even despite evidence to the contrary. In other words, beliefs are not necessarily facts! Yet, in our mind they are fact; usually because we acquired them as children before we had reasoning powers. We believed whatever adults told us. We didn't question that our religious beliefs were true. If we were born in the 13th century we didn't doubt that the world was flat and people couldn't fly, in a vehicle that is.

Wars have been fought over people's beliefs. Millions of people have been exterminated because of the religious fanaticism or ideologies of some cult who were so sure that they were right. What we were so positive was true at one time, we now know was false, both personally and globally. How do we really know what to believe? How can we possibly know what is true? We can't.

How we form beliefs

As we experience life through our five senses, (sight, sound, feel, smell, taste) we form representations of the world. One never really knows the truth, only our interpretation. So, one adult child of an alcoholic proclaims, "Of course I'm an alcoholic. My parents were alcoholics, what do you expect?" While the sibling affirms, "Of course I don't drink. My parents were alcoholics, what do you expect?" Two children, same family, yet very different perceptions of what it meant to be the child of an alcoholic. Leaving them with very definite expectations for their life which they lived up to, right?

Another way to say it is: it's not what happens, it's how we interpret the event. A little boy who got beat by his father may reason, "Bad boys get beat, therefore I am bad, therefore, I am not lovable." Imagine how that will impact his life. A little girl is sexually molested and grows up thinking she is bad. While most of our self-concept is formed by the age of eight, we continue to be imprinted by people and events into our teens, maybe later. Roy, (#5), was a first-generation Japanese American. He was raised in poverty. That gave him a very different reality than I had. He was only 14 when his family was put in the concentration (relocation) camp. When he was released after the war, he was confronted with horrific bigotry and prejudice that had not been there before he left. He joined the army, as thousands of Japanese Americans did during WWII. Servicemen were brainwashed to dehumanize the enemy, the 'Japs'. How else could they kill them? Roy's representation was that he was inferior and thus not lovable. Yet, not all of his 8 siblings, nor tens-of-thousands of other Japanese Americans who were interned, grew up thinking they are not lovable.

Michelle's father, and then her step-father, deserted her mother for younger women. They also managed to hide their wealth and leave the family in near poverty while they went on to live a life of luxury with their young wives. Imagine how that would make you feel. What would you believe about yourself if two husbands left you for other women? In fact, why did she marry the second one? She already had a subconscious expectation that men were always unfaithful cads. Maybe, her RAS was working perfectly to draw her to the cads. I know Michelle's was. Michelle had been in a long-term relationship with a guy who was not capable of commitment. She was bright, educated and looked like a Barbie Doll. She swore the only guys in nightclubs were cads, just like her fathers. It took very little to change her expectations. Before a year had passed Michelle was in love with a wonderful, loving man. They lived happily ever after.

I have two friends whose husbands avoid making love to them, yet spend their evenings in the garage watching porn. What representation would you make about yourself if you were them? That is so damn degrading! I feel their pain and I just want to go kick the shit out of those bastard husbands.

If you believe that you are not smart because you lack education, you are going to miss a lot of opportunities. I never even applied for any job that paid over minimum wage until I was 27 because of that limiting belief. I love the story of Victor Seribriakoff in Zig Ziegler's book "See You at the Top". When Victor was 15 his teacher told him that he was too dumb to finish school. She advised him to go to trade school and get a job. Victor took that advice and for the next 17 years he worked as an itinerant worker on various odd jobs. But when he was 32 an amazing thing happened, an evaluation showed that Victor had an IQ of 161. (Average is 95-105). Suddenly, his whole life changed, he became a successful businessman and secured a number of patents and has written a number of books. Imagine that; for 17 years Victor thought he was dumb and acted dumb and all of a sudden, he began acting like the genius he always was.

What unconscious representations or beliefs do you have that are limiting you? You'll begin to find out soon, if you haven't already. Some are easily uncovered, some not. In fact, changing them is easy compared to finding them.

How we shed beliefs

> "Man is born believing. A man bears belief like a
> tree bears apples." Ralph Waldo Emerson

When we are children we believe we can be and do anything- rock stars, astronauts, ballerinas. Then about the time we learn that the fat

63

man in the red fur suit is really Daddy, we begin hearing disparaging remarks about our dreams, possibilities, and abilities.

- "Get your head out of the clouds."
- "You've got delusions of grandeur."
- "You're not talented, like Madonna."
- "You're not special, like Oprah."
- "Don't get uppity."
- "Where'd you get that hifalutin idea?"
- "Don't get too big for your breeches."
- "Get off your high horse."
- "Don't bite off more than you can chew."
- "Don't be a pipe dreamer."
- "Don't be a Pollyanna."

"BE REALISTIC!"

In other words, "Just who do you think you are, anyway?" These are the adults you trust. They know you, so it must be true. You aren't special. So now we're all grown up and when we think of doing something other than what is 'expected' there is a little voice inside that says, "Just who do you think you are anyway? You can't do that, be realistic.". And proceeds to give you all the reasons why.

- Why you don't have enough experience.
- You need more training. Funny thing- I had more success in my first month in real estate and I didn't have a clue what I was doing.
- She won't pay that much for your services. So, you hold yourself back from raising your rates.
- It isn't the right time. You should wait until the kids are in school, out of school, etc.
- No one wants to hear what you have to say. The fraud syndrome.

- You're not ready. No one ever is!
- Why you only have a 9th grade education, who's going to listen to you? I have had clients with Master's Degrees that thought this.
- You don't have the right credentials. There will always be someone with more.
- You're not good enough (smart enough, thin enough, fill-in-the-blank enough)
- You're not lovable. So, you don't deserve that great guy.
- You're just not enough.

Imagine hearing any of those disparaging and discouraging remarks at 7 or 8 years old. You believe everything you are told. You haven't developed reasoning yet. So, it is fact, you should not expect to have, be or do what you had wanted. "Get off your high horse." "Be realistic!" So, the answer to "Who do you think you are?" becomes, "Why, I'm nobody. Nobody at all." Can you feel that? I do. God forbid, we think we are special. Don't have a good self-esteem. That won't get you to heaven. For Pete's' sake. My 90-year-old mother told me, "Daddy was real proud of you when you opened your own real estate school." That was news to me. Why couldn't either of them tell me they were proud of me as a child, or an adult? Why couldn't they make me feel good about myself? It was what they learned from their parents, and their parents learned it from their parents, etc. A young groom was curious, so he asked his new bride, "Why do you always cut both ends of the roast off before you bake it?" "I'm not sure. My mother always did it." She asked her mother, "Why do you cut the ends of the roast before you bake it?" Mother replied, "I don't know, my mother always did it." So, the young bride asked her grandmother, "Grandma, why do you and Mom always cut the ends off the roast before you bake it?" Grandma replied, "Well, I don't know why your mother does it, but I do it because my pan is too small."

Sayings, proverbs and adages that we grew up with formed our beliefs about how things work. An adage is a saying that becomes widely accepted as truth over time. Adages are usually observances of life and behavior that express a general truth. While they are meant to impart sage advice: "Look before you leap." "Do not judge a man until you have walked a mile in his shoes.". Many just create unnecessary limits in our lives. Think about these two: "A bird in the hand is better than two in the bush." "Better the devil you know than the one you don't." In other words, it could be worse, so better not make waves. Settle and be content with what you have. I've heard women advise their daughters to stay in abusive marriages because they took this adage as absolute fact. When I begged Daddy not to make me marry Lloyd at 14, he said, "You made your bed, now you'll have to lie in it." Come on, what a terribly destructive way to think, especially when it applies to the rest of your life. He sure wanted to get rid of me. My parents never knew that my sisters and I were all being abused by our husbands. We were told that we should not let the family know if our husband did something bad because, although we would forgive him, the family won't forgive and forget. It may sound crazy when you apply it to something that could be life threatening but, our beliefs are not logical. Usually, we don't even have a clue where the belief came from, it just is. For us, it is true.

There are many common phrases from around the world that warn of the dangers of high expectations or reaching beyond your 'limitations'. A popular Dutch aphorism is, "The tallest poppy gets cut down." The Japanese proverb *Deru kugi utareru* — "The nail that sticks out gets hammered down" which not only refers to being too ambitious, but *anyone* who fails to conform. Again, warning us that it is not safe to aspire to have or be more than our peers.

You may feel the pain right now, just reading that. And, I'll bet you can add to this list and later you will. Now you can begin to see where you got your corrupted self-concept that made you feel unworthy.

How many more can you think of? You may think sayings like that didn't impact you, but they did. I'll bet your family had a favorite. (I'd love to add it to my next book). A Jewish man in my workshop had the AH HA when he realized his family had a Yiddish saying, 'Gonsig k'nacker', that basically translated into, "Mister Big-shot". When Mike wanted to be more than average, it was considered an insult to his father. He'd be told something like, "Your father made a perfectly good living working at the factory. Who do you think you are, Mr. Big Shot?" It was meant to make him feel ashamed that he wanted more. It had haunted him, (unconsciously) all his life and was preventing him from reaching his potential.

<u>Conform or be abandoned</u>

Conformity is the key to happiness because it is the *only* way to be accepted by the tribe. Human beings re not autonomous. We need to be part of a pack. For that to happen we must be liked and accepted. If you are different you could be ostracized and abandoned. So, we emulate our peers in every way. We dress like them, vacation like them, drive similar cars. If your tribe are cowboys, you won't be aspiring to own an Infiniti. You'll want the hottest pick-up in the parish.

If you're blue collar, your vacation dream might be camping at Yosemite or a dream trip to Disney World. Your bucket list won't include Paris, Venice and Amsterdam. For one thing, you won't believe it is possible and our dreams are limited by what we believe is possible. But, the other thing is, that your friends won't relate to you going to Europe. They will think you are highfalutin. I can't talk to my family about touring France or going to South America, they've never been, and don't aspire to go. Besides, they think I am being hifalutin. We want to be around like-minded souls, our Tribe.

Of course, not all children heard those things in their family. I'm sure Bill Gates or J. Paul Getty didn't pass on limiting expectations for their children. Quite the opposite, their kids were *expected* to get a degree and be successful. The kid's peers at the private schools they attended had the same expectations. Lucky them. Roy and I expected our daughter, Tiffany, to get a degree and be successful. She was a $6-figure woman before she was 30.

We wouldn't have heard of Oprah if her only expectations came from TV, or even real life, role models. Her grandmother convinced her that she could become anything she wanted to become. Most of us didn't have someone in our life who believed in our possibilities. Far from it. For sure, most of us never dreamed of getting rich.

Not that there is anything wrong with being middle-class. That's the 3rd level of the pyramid, 'Acceptance'. Most people stay there. But, you want more, don't you? You're not going to be afraid to be abandoned by your tribe because you know there is another tribe you can join.

I am not saying you should be discontent if you do not have lofty goals. You should aspire to have the life of your dreams. Whatever that is. My sister and brother-in-law left the Silicon Valley rat race and retired to a simple life in rural Bossier, Louisiana, on three acres of land. They have wonderful neighbors, no financial stress, and are completely contented. It is a wonderful life and provides everything they want and need. That is success! On the other hand, I want to travel the world, have expensive jewelry and a maid. I wanted to be super successful and, I never reached many of my goals. I can't afford all that I want, but, even though I am not satisfied, I am contented and grateful. So, who's better off, me or Pat? I think we both are. I'm doing what is right for me and she is doing what is right for her.

> "Ah, but a man's reach should exceed his grasp, Or what's a heaven for?" Robert Browning

TRANSFORMATION EXPLORATION 8: SAYINGS AND ADAGES
Circle any of the above sayings or beliefs that you felt some energy around.

You may easily remember many things you heard as a child, like some of the above, and think, "Oh, I get it! That's why I'm screwed up." But, it isn't that simple. It's the things that you will dredge up from deep within your unconscious that will have the biggest impact on 'who you think you are'.

PART II: POSITIVE INTENTIONS

Most limiting beliefs that we inherited were meant to be for our own good. There was a positive intent to keeping our expectations in check. In some convoluted way, they wanted to protect us. They didn't want us to get our hopes up and be disappointed. They wanted us to be happy with what we had, or what they thought we could have in life. A mother in an abusive marriage may tell her daughter all men are devils, don't trust them, don't let your heart be broken, don't dare to love. The daughter sees proof of this in her own father.

I know my mother meant well when I was 12 years old, and fully developed, and she told me, "Boys are only interested in one thing from you." Obviously, she hoped this would keep me a virgin. But, of course, the results were quite different. Sex became a tool to get love. I thought if I was good in bed, men would love me. Of course, the 60's compounded that belief. When we women were liberated by the pill we had the freedom to be as promiscuous as men had been. For many women sex became a natural part of dating. Then, women began to realize that we didn't enjoy casual sex without relationship, and things changed, thank God. But, I still thought the way for me to win a man was with sex. After all, what else did I have going for me? And, to me the ultimate proof that I was lovable was if a man wanted to marry me. Even though John stood by me through a 60-pound weight gain, cancer and a mastectomy, until recently, I was still not 100% convinced that I was lovable, despite the evidence. Logically I knew it, but those deeply held, unconscious beliefs, take a lot of work to eradicate. Writing my story helped convince me.

TRANSFORMATION EXPLORATION 9: WORDS THAT HIT HOME

Using a separate page for each one
1. Write out four (or more) things you heard or were told as a child?
2. What expectation did you form as a result?
3. What has it prevented you from achieving?
4. What was the positive intent?

PART III: CHANGE YOUR STORY-CHANGE YOUR LIFE

We all have our stories. Our 'story' is what we have been telling ourselves for years about how we got in this mess. Some of it is fact, some of it is the result of deletions, distortions and generalizations. Mostly, it is how we interpreted or, misinterpreted, our life experiences. Have you ever been dead sure you remembered something from your childhood just because you heard someone tell the 'story' over and over? That's what we do.

This book is not my autobiography, although many fans have requested it. This book is about your story, how it evolves throughout these Transformation Explorations, and how you evolve. However, I need to share enough of my own story to illustrate my 10 keys. I think the examples will give you insight into your own life. You can begin writing your life story anytime. It will be an amazing, transformative journey.

Compared to other women's stories, your Crazy Aunt Carole's is not very dramatic, but it is colorful. My story used to be, 'I was the helpless victim of abusive men.' Oh, there's no question, I was abused. I was sexually molested, by various men, including several doctors, starting at around three years old and ending well into my thirties. As a teenager, I hooked up with many hoodlums and lowlifes. One kidnapped me at gunpoint. Another drugged and raped me. One charmer rolled the car, with me in it, trying to outrun the police. Three robbed my parents. At 13, I started abusing alcohol and had my first run-in with the police. I was a bad girl, and the black sheep of the family. I was beaten, cheated on, and otherwise betrayed, by my husbands. I couldn't help it. After all, I was born with a deformed right arm that severely limited my ability to work and I only had a ninth-grade education. I knew I was too dumb to get a decent job. I needed a man to take care of me. In fact, I believed I was nothing without a man.

But, 'Victim' is an old story. It isn't who I am today. I still love having a man in my life. I don't suppose that will ever change. But, I won't wither away if John, my husband of 23 years, goes first. I'm no longer helpless and I'm certainly not dumb. So much of what I believed to be the absolute truth, changed in the process of writing my own story. It will happen for you too. Let me begin by introducing you to Eve and Glinda, my alter-egos.

Eve is insecure, needy, helpless, and often low-class. Eve believes I am meant for a life of strife and struggle. She doubts I am lovable and chooses men who confirm it. She sabotages me every time I gain success. She is the lower version of myself. She says, "You could never do that. Just who do you think you are, anyway, Oprah?"

Glinda is my higher self. She is poised, sophisticated, and confident. She knows I was destined for greater things and she makes it happen. Glinda knows I am lovable, just the way I am- fat and imperfect. When Eve knocks me down, Glinda comes to my rescue, after a while. Glinda is my authentic self and it was a battle for her to win dominance and let me claim the woman I was meant to be. Glinda says, "Go for it Carole. You deserve it!"

My Leave it to Beaver' Childhood

I was born in in 1945. (Gads, I'm practically an antique!) My mother, Irene, was 5 feet tall and 110 pounds with slender hips. I was a chubby 9-pound baby that could not make it through the birth canal. After 36 hours of labor the doctor had to pull me out thereby damaging my brachial plexus nerve. This left me with limited use of my right arm. My father, Art, was an entrepreneur and real estate investor. He bought run-down houses that we lived in while he and Mom fixed them up. We moved about every 9 months to a year for most of my life, except for six years when I was in elementary school when we settled in West Portal, an upper-middle-class neighborhood of San Francisco. Daddy went into the juke box business with my maternal grandfather and, while we were not rich, we were comfortable. It was a wonderful, 'Leave it to Beaver' life. Daddy was the breadwinner. Mommy was a homemaker. Summer vacation was spent camping at a resort on the Russian River. That was the middle-class Riviera in the fifties.

My sister Patty was three years younger than me. She and I were great playmates until I hit adolescence and my interest turned to boys. She was a good girl. Jeanie, was four years my senior. She was smart and sweet and had a natural poise about her. Even as a child, she was timid and shy. Mom and Dad thought she was the model daughter, albeit a little shy. She never gave them any trouble or heartache. As I grew into an unruly teenager, I was compared to 'Miss Perfect' often. "Why can't you be more like Jeanie? She never gave us any trouble." I am blessed that my sisters and I are still very close. I was almost the opposite of timid Jeanie. I was bold, gregarious, and popular. When I was five and Jeanie nine, we got lost in our new neighborhood. Jeanie was scared and crying. I said, "Don't worry Jeanie, I'll get us home." I knocked on a stranger's door and they helped us get home. I was fearless. When I was nine my best friend, Gloria, and I decided it was time to be on our own. We packed two hot dogs and buns and rode our bikes to Ocean Beach, (about three miles) where we were going to live on fish. I *hate* fish and had no clue how we would catch them or cook them. Not a very well laid out plan. When we got hungry, we tried to steal an apple but chickened out and headed home. Unfortunately, we got lost and didn't find our way home until almost 9pm. Our parents were frantic. The police had issued an APB (All Points Bulletin) for us. I was taken to the police station to explain myself and sent to bed without dinner. Gloria's parents fed and pampered her. I thought she was lucky to have been adopted as she always got spoiled.

I was a born leader. When I was eight I founded the 'Four Leaf Clover' club. Wanting to be democratic, I suggested we elect officers. When they, (all the girls I had recruited) elected someone else president, I disbanded the club. The nerve! I wrote and starred in a skit about Christmas greed and I sang in the talent contest. I wanted to be a cross between Annie Oakley, (who could out-shoot an out-ride any man and took no guff!), Our Miss Brooks (the school teacher on the sitcom of the same name), and Jan Morrow, Doris Day's role as the glamorous interior designer in 'Pillow Talk', also starring Rock Hudson who I wanted to grow up and marry. Boy, was I disappointed to find out he was gay! I also wanted to marry Gene Autry. I guess I was fickle.

Mom was a superb homemaker and the best mother in the world. She loved being domestic. She was subservient and was an obedient helpmate. That's what good women were in the 50s. Realistically, I expected to grow up and be just like her, and June Cleaver, and love it! Daddy adored Mommy and showered her with affection and gifts. It was so romantic. He was gentle and kind. It all looked so perfect. Neither of my parents drank and neither would say shit if they had a mouthful. In other words, they were perfect. So was I, then. I was happy and didn't have a care in the world. I was Glinda.

The real story

So, wouldn't you think that with a father image like my dad, my two sisters and I would marry men like him? Well, we did, but not in the way we wanted. You see, what we didn't realize until I did the work in this book, was that, while Daddy worshiped Mommy and smothered her with attention, us girls got none of that. I can't remember a hug. He never said, "I love you. He never said, "Hey Kiddo, you're talented, you're smart, you're going to do great things." He certainly never let me think that someday some wonderful man would love me. In fact, everything revolved around Mom. He wasn't mean, just indifferent, which contributed to us girls feeling that we were somehow, less lovable. Daddy came home from work, sat in his easy chair and read the paper.

I doubt Daddy had any desire to have children. In fact, I remember Mom saying, "Children are the domain of women. Men are not interested in them." Here's something that came up for me a few years ago when all the children were massacred at an elementary school in Cincinnati. I was bewildered to see men grieving for children that weren't even their own. I never realized I had an unconscious belief that men didn't care about children. I wonder what breakthrough you are having about your own childhood.

So, my sisters and myself married men who, for the most part, had no desire for children and pretty much ignored them when we had them. Worse yet, we married men who made us feel inadequate and unlovable. They cheated on us and/or were abusive in other ways. Oddly, Father would never have done that to Mom. But, that's how screwed up our representations get. It wasn't the romantic figure that we consciously saw, that we attracted, it was the man who neglected us and made us feel like our needs were unimportant

As you write your own story I encourage you to discuss it with your siblings. You'll be stunned at the revelations that come up.

I think, as I got older, Daddy saw that I was getting in the way of Mom's happiness. To that, he was right. I had hurt her. It broke her heart to see me getting into trouble. Father was very protective of her. She could do no wrong. If Mom and I had a dispute, I was not even allowed to voice my case. She was right, and that was that. I was not important. My happiness didn't matter. Dad was very close to his mother who had been widowed twice while he was just a child and had struggled to survive. He has a deep respect for women.

Here's the thing- It's a father's job to make his daughters feel loved and worthy. As my story evolved, and I shared my realizations with my sisters, I remembered more and more times that my father made me feel unlovable. But, you know what I have realized, I also made him feel unlovable. Even as a child, I wanted more. I wanted a mansion and maid. I admired other men, wealthy men. To me, rich men had class, (meaning, he didn't). This made Daddy feel inadequate. He wanted to be my hero, as he was Mom's. No matter how many times he failed, she still idolized him. Looking back, I realize Daddy did love us girls. He just didn't know how to express it- probably because he hadn't had a role model himself.

I can also see now, how my family tried to cure me of my unladylike qualities: assertiveness, tenacity, ambition, thinking for myself. I can even remember my little sister, Patty, telling me, "Carole Jo, you'll never get a husband. You're too domineering." We were probably 6 and 9 at the time. She may not have used those exact words, but that is what was imprinted in my brain. I was not lovable as my authentic go-getter self. I can't tell you how many times I rewrote my story to arrive at that truth, but it was many. My sisters and I got little praise. In fact, Mom was raised to believe, "pride cometh before the fall." God forbid I should be proud of my accomplishments, or my looks. That would be sinful. Of course, they could only pass on their own beliefs.

When I was 10, the juke box business was sold. Dad got a real estate license and did quite well in the beginning, then tanked. He tried selling insurance and once again, started with a bang, then tanked. It mirrored my careers.

Mom, who hadn't worked in twenty years, reluctantly had to get a job. She brushed up on her high school typing and shorthand and went to work as a clerk-typist. Daddy promised it was only temporary. She worked until she was 85. Daddy struggled the rest of his life with finances and success.

Eve Emerged

That's me when I graduated from the 6th grade at 12. I thought I was as homely as a mud-rat. I was huge. At 5'7" I towered over the other adolescents. I weighed 145 and wore a 38-D. I hated my big breasts. (Having children took care of that problem.) I remember the frustration of trying to find an outfit when I had to go on stage to accept an award for two pieces I entered in a state-wide art contest. I was a child but had to buy a woman's dress. That wonderful childhood was soon to end.

In April of the 7th grade, my world changed. I changed. Eve invaded my persona. Daddy couldn't get back on his feet and he lost the family home. He stayed with Grandma in Silicon Valley while he looked for work. Jeanie, now a high-school senior, moved in with our cousin to finish school, and Mom, Patty and I, moved into an apartment in the slums of the City, Hunters Point, which was 90% black. And they weren't the Cosbys. They were hoods and thugs and gang members who carried weapons, and used them.

Within weeks of moving, I got hit by a car and was thrown 60 feet, landing face down on the pavement. I was in a comma for 10 days, hospitalized for 6 weeks, then bedridden for several more. My father moved in the apartment temporarily to care for me. I didn't recognize it at the time, but he was depressed. I overheard him, on more than one occasion, complaining about having to take off work to care for me. But, I don't think he had a job yet. We barely spoke. I felt like a terrible burden.

By the time I could walk it was summer, school was out, and I turned 13. I had only attended the local junior high a few weeks, so I had no friends. I was lonely, so I walked up and down 3rd Street looking for companionship. Mind you, I didn't look 13. In fact, the ambulance driver had estimated my age as 18. I met Elena, a 13-year-old Puerto Rican girl who taught me how to fit in. That meant: smoke, drink, look like a slut, carry brass knuckles and shoplift. There, now I fit in- at least on the outside. That's Eve below. Can you believe the transformation in me in only six months?

The next 'companion' I met was a middle-aged Hispanic man who took me to his dank basement apartment and molested me. A college boy also molested me. The peculiar thing is, I have no memory of the details and I didn't think I had intercourse. In my 30s, I discovered that I had been molested by various men from the time I was three years old and had buried the memories. I guess that's because I felt so dirty and ashamed that I had participated in the acts. Since that time, memories of molestation have surfaced, like my girlfriends' father playing doctor with us when we were eight or nine years old. But, to this day, I can't remember being penetrated, although I know I was.

My first official date was with two 23-year old carpenters that I picked up on 3rd Street. My mother allowed me to go out with them.

They told her we were double dating for a movie. Only they never picked up another girl. Mom was very naive. They tried to rape me, then literally, gave me bus fare and dropped me off. (It wasn't the last time I got lucky. I hitchhiked often as a teenager.) The next lowlifes I picked up, robbed my parents. My father was furious with me. He never forgave me for allowing these scumbags to steal Mom's precious saxophone that she had played in an all-girl orchestra in the 30s, before they got married. I didn't like myself much either. More shame, more guilt. I was no good.

"I deeply and completely love and accept myself. I deeply and completely love and accept myself. I deeply and completely love and accept myself."

First Love

I started 8th grade and a very weird thing happened. The cutest boy in school, one of the few white boys, got a crush on me. At first, I couldn't believe it, then, we started going steady. I was in love and oh, so happy. But, that was not to last either.

Back to civilization

Unfortunately, my parents had realized what a disaster that move to Hunter's Point was, and Daddy dragged me off to stay at Grandmas with him. I was devastated. I was ripped away from the first person to love me. Soon Dad found a blue-collar job working for a vending company and the family reunited in a cheap rental in Silicon Valley next door to my cousins. Mom commuted to San Francisco for her job as a clerk-typist. Now, I was expected to fit in with the innocent adolescents in my 8th grade class. Mom scraped the makeup off me and made me dye my bleached hair back to brown, as if that would make me a normal teen. It was too late for that. As soon as I was out the door, the make-up was reapplied. I looked 18. I smoked and drank like a sailor. I was anything but normal. I was the black sheep of the family, and I knew it. My own cousins weren't allowed to hang around with me. I believed that I was bad to the core. I became a bully. I wanted to fit in, but I just didn't.

Naturally, it didn't take long for me to find the other 'black sheep'. I was still 13 when I arrived home from an all-night drinking party and the police were waiting for me. Mom took me to the doctor to see if I had had sex. The doctor felt me up and gave me a pelvic exam, then told my mother, I was not a virgin. I swore that was not true because, to my knowledge, I had never had intercourse. I also didn't realize that the doctor had abused me by feeling my breast. The first of several doctors to do inappropriate things to me. How powerful the mind is at hiding things we can't bear to remember.

The real story

I wasn't a bad seed, hopelessly doomed to a lowly life. I was conforming the best I knew how to get acceptance and approval, which I dearly needed. No one ever told me I was a good girl or that I had potential for anything other than cleaning toilets. In fact, pedophiles who molested me, told me I was nasty. It was as if there was a part of me that was evil. Eve was in control. Glinda was ashamed. Thus began the dichotomy of my life.

In fairness, my parents did the best they could. They were good people. My mother was an angel. However, when boys gave me attention, she feared it would turn my head, so she asked me, "What makes you think you're so lovable? You're not special." I think I got married to prove I was lovable. See Mom, somebody does love me.

By the end of the eighth grade, I had lost the tough girl persona, but was still wild. I dated older boys, mostly high-school drop-outs with cars. I was in constant trouble and caused my parents no end of grief. My two sisters were good girls. What happened to Carole Jo? My father didn't seem to like me at all.

Child Bride

At 14, I finally found a clean-cut boyfriend who my parents liked. Lloyd was a sweet, immature 18-year-old from Oklahoma. When he proposed, I was thrilled. I was anxious to be a homemaker, and mother. My father decided this was a good way to get me out of the house, so I wouldn't hurt Mother anymore. Before I knew it, I was in front of a judge getting consent to marry at such a young age. Two weeks later I was dressed in my 8th grade graduation dress, ready to walk down the aisle. I begged Daddy not to make me get married. I wasn't ready. He said, "You made your bed, now you have to lie in it." I cried all the way down the aisle.

A few weeks later Lloyd lost his job as a night janitor. That's when we discovered he was illiterate. He couldn't find work so, in the dead of winter, along with his pregnant sister, her ex-con husband and their three-year-old daughter, we moved to Detroit. I got a job as a car hop and I was the only one in the household that worked. Two months later I was in protective custody in juvenile hall because my teenage groom was beating me up. Poor Carole Jo. That was my victim story.

The real story

In reality, it was more like two kids duking it out. I may have even hit first. Maybe. I was no more ready to be a wife and mother (God forbid) than a 10-year-old playing house. That's really what we were doing, playing house.

My parents had to take me back. Once again, I promised to be a good little teenager and conform. That was not possible. Now, I had been an adult with no rules. Curfews were for kids, not me. Eve was right back to my old shenanigans, drinking and staying out late with bad boys.

No Convent for This Girl

By the time I turned 15 in June, (six months later), my mother was at her wits end. She wanted to save me. I overheard a phone conversation she had with my aunt. Mom was planning to send me to the Good Sheppard Convent for Wayward Girls until I turned 18. Are you kidding? Me, in a convent? We weren't even Catholic! The next night, one of my boyfriends was waiting outside at midnight. I was so afraid my father would wake up and catch me that my knees turned to water. I had to crawl out to the front door leaving behind my suitcase. I grabbed the box of extra clothes that I had hid in the bushes, and ran to his car.

I took a Greyhound bus to Long Beach where another boyfriend set me up in a hotel. The next day I got a driver's permit that said I was 23 years old and that my name was Joanne Holiday. A day later, I had a job at a small hamburger joint. Within a week, I was managing the place. I was the sole employee; I opened, closed and, did the banking. There was a naval station and sailors flocked to my joint to flirt with me. I was having a ball. I'd say Glinda was in good form. But, at night, Eve flourished as I hung out in bars with a sordid crowd.

After about 6 weeks Glinda fell in love with an adorable sailor and decided to marry him. I went to the bar to inform the bartender, who I had been casually dating. The next thing I remembered was being roughly shook awake by a cop. I was naked. I was arrested and spent 3 days in Long Beach County Jail where I was interrogated for hours each day by District Attorneys, FBI and DEA. It turns out, the feds had been after Mr. Bartender for some time for various nefarious endeavors, including racketeering and drugs. They wanted me to testify that I had sex with him, so they could get him for statutory rape. The charges against me were: Sexual Delinquency and being Incorrigible. Can you imagine having your teenage daughter arrested for having sex or being incorrigible today? I was treated like a common tramp and criminal. No one thought to test me for the date-rape drug. They assumed I had gone willingly. I thought I just got drunk and deserved the rape. I was so groggy I didn't know what was going on. Now I realize, I had been drugged. I refused to testify. I spent four months in the San Jose Juvenile Hall while the well-meaning authorities conspired with my parents to imprison me until I turned 18. Luckily, CYA (California Youth Authority) said I wasn't 'bad' enough. Well, yeah, what was my crime? The convent said I was too "worldly". LOL

The real story.

The reason I ran away was because my mother was going to have me locked up for three years. That didn't matter to Daddy. He wrote to me in juvenile hall and said, "Your mother cried herself to sleep every night. I tried to hate you, but I couldn't." I was devastated. He didn't say he loved me, just that he didn't hate me. At the time, no one realized I had been drugged and raped. They wouldn't have believed it anyway. I resented being treated like a criminal just because I didn't want to be locked up. Mom called me a tramp.

Husband # 2, Charming Lothario

I turned 16 in Juvi. My parents were stuck with the bad apple again. I really did try to be good. But I was out in bars most nights, dancing and flirting, and drinking way too much, then to my everlasting shame, driving home. I was working at a Big Box store and was dependable and trustworthy. Funny, I never got any credit for my positive qualities, only my flaws. It wasn't long before I got swept off my feet by a charming Lothario. Skip told me he was 23, he was actually 18. He told me I was his first wife. I was his third, and he hadn't bothered to divorce one of them. He talked me into eloping just four weeks after we met. I knew it was a mistake, but I had gone all the way with him, (something I rarely did), and he told me he would dump me if I didn't marry him. How dumb was that? Then, so my parents couldn't annul the marriage, Skip talked me into making sure I was pregnant. He loved me so much, he couldn't bear the thought of losing me. Six weeks later, I was heaving my guts up and Skip had abandoned ship. A girl came to my work and claimed she was engaged to Skip. I was devastated. I had lost the love of my life. I swallowed 75 aspirin and almost died. I also found out he already had a child that he wasn't supporting. This is how stupid I was, while they pumped my stomach, I was afraid they would pump the baby out. I'm not kidding! I had Heidi one month after I turned 17.

So, my story was, 'I was a helpless victim of another scoundrel who betrayed me'. At least that was my story for decades.

The real story

I barely knew Skip. We were two horny kids looking for love and our 'happily ever after'. If he hadn't dumped me, I would've been bored in no time and left him. I blamed him and hated him all those years.

It turns out Heidi found him when she was 50 and they formed a great relationship. He is a nice man after all, although, at 74, he admits that, even through six marriages, he remained a womanizer.

<u>Husband #3 Rambling Romeo</u>

While pregnant, I earned my keep by cooking, grocery shopping and cleaning house for my parents. After Heidi was born I was on welfare for a while. It was hard to work for $2 and hour and pay $.75 cents for babysitters. I needed a husband. Now, my parents were stuck with me and a baby. When Heidi was nine months old, I met another charmer in a nightclub. Ernie was a sun-bronzed carpenter who drove a new candy apple red caddie, had a speed boat and raced stock cars. He was a man's' man. He was also a womanizer. He cheated constantly for the year we dated. Then I married him. It didn't stop. I left him over and over and he would romance me back. Then, during a brief reconciliation, I stupidly got pregnant. Two weeks before Kimberly was born, Ernie came home at 4 am, swearing his derby-car trailer had a flat tire. When I went to do laundry, there was lipstick all over his collar, and lower. I called him at his mother's house, where he spent most of his time. I was screaming hysterically and told his mother what he had done. I guess she gave him a lecture because he stopped cheating. I was finally able to stay home and be a housewife and mommy. But, I hated the fact that his mother made all his decisions for him. She was even the beneficiary on his life insurance policy. A marriage counselor said he had never seen a worse Oedipus complex. I wasn't about to let his mother rule me. I was sure the grass was greener somewhere else, so I finally filed for divorce. Ernie was heart-broken.

After he moved back with his mother, while I was out one night, Ernie called and told my babysitter that he had a gun and that he was going to kill me. He said, "No one else would ever have me." He meant it! When I came home early the next morning, he was waiting. When I saw the red caddy pull into the carport behind me, I looked down at my nylons and garter belt on the seat beside me, me and took off like a bat out hell in my little Falcon station wagon. He chased me through the neighborhood waving a gun, until I pulled into the police station parking lot honking my horn. He eventually accepted the divorce. The sad part is, Heidi thought Ernie was her daddy. She couldn't understand why Daddy picked up Kim on weekends and took her to see Grandma and Grandpa, but left her behind. OMG, that was, and still is, heart wrenching. Finally, I decided both my daughters would be better off if Ernie had custody of Kim, or rather his mother had custody, for she raised Kim. Kim was the only child, grandchild and great grandchild and was spoiled rotten. I had her every weekend.

My story was, 'He was a loser that betrayed me and broke my heart. He was a mama's boy and I lost respect for him. Poor victim, me.'

The real story

Once Ernie stopped cheating, I was bored. It was the constant drama and excitement of the fighting and then him winning me back, that kept me stimulated. I also realize that, while I was attracted to him and we had fun together, I wasn't really in love with him. How could I have been, when I fell out of love? He was a wonderful man. There were over 200 people at his funeral and flowers out to the street. Too bad he fell in love with me. He was the victim in the end. He never remarried and died in a motorcycle accident at 37. I expected 9-year-old Kim to come live with me and my new husband, but Grandma told her, "If you leave me, Grandpa and I will die." How's that for manipulation? Kim remained with Grandma and eventually moved her boyfriend in. When, after 5 years, she got married, Grandma gave Kim the lot next door and the money to build a home so she could keep running Kim's life. After Grandma was widowed, she moved in with Kim and her husband, and ruined their marriage just as she had mine and Ernie's. My mother-in-law was not an evil woman, she was filling her own need for love and connection that she lacked in her loveless marriage.

Husband #4 Cheating Casanova

Now what? I needed to find a way to support myself and Heidi. I found I could carry a tray of drinks with my good arm and set them down with the gimpy one, so I became a cocktail waitress, and supplemented my meager wages with food stamps and rent subsidy. It was fun in the beginning, but not a good occupation for a gal who loved to drink. Nor, was it a job that gave me opportunities to find my next Mr. Right. Who wants to hang around bars waiting for the half-drunk waitress to dry glasses at 2:30 in the morning? Drunks and bartenders. One such man, a handsome Hispanic, alcoholic, who bartended part-time, insinuated himself into my life. Chuck was a charmer and, he gave me my first orgasm. That was a strong hold on me. However, he started beating me up shortly after we got involved. He gave me STDs on several occasions. I broke it off many times over the three-year relationship, but couldn't find a replacement, so I finally married him. More stupidity, right? The abuse got worse. Finally, he framed me for attempted murder, and he had two cop friends who swore they witnessed it. I spent 3 nights in the felony ward of the local jail and was released on bail. It was a nightmare that haunted me for decades. After eight weeks, that seemed like years, he dropped the charges. I finally had to move on. You can imagine how that story went, 'He was another loser and I was a helpless victim again.'

The real story

While Chuck was undeniably, horribly abusive to me. This doesn't seem to be who he really is. Chuck was the lower alter-ego of Carlos. You might say, for the six years we were together, I brought out this lower self. He was a good man in many ways. He was law abiding, dependable and honest, if you don't count infidelity. (That sounds ridiculous, doesn't it?) He was very good to my girls and years later, gave Heidi away at her wedding. While we were together, he refused to even accept a promotion to manager at the grocery store where he clerked. On the other hand, in his early twenties, he had married, and owned a business and a home. This was Charlie, his higher self. Unfortunately, he lost it all, including his three kids, due to his infidelity. (The man was definitely over-sexed. He was insatiable.) Oddly, he even used the different variations of his name, Chuck and Charlie during those times.

After our divorce, Chuck became Charlie again. He married a lovely Hispanic woman, bought a liquor store, a home, raised her three kids, and lived happily ever after. I can only assume he did not treat her as he had me. You may not think that is possible, because, as my mother always said, "A leopard doesn't change his stripes.". But I have seen different. I know how I contributed to his behavior. You see, unconsciously, he had to know, that even though I married him, I didn't really love him. He won me by default. I didn't respect him and admire him, and he lived down to my expectations. He needed me to leave him because he couldn't leave me. He needed to find a woman who would bring out Charlie. And, he did.

<u>My first career</u>

While I was married to Chuck, Glinda was dominant. I worked in a dress store for minimum wage. (By the way, when I was married,

I put aside the Party Girl and curtailed my drinking to a cocktail a day.) I did not want to go back to the bar life that Glinda hated (and Eve loved). I wondered what a gal with a ninth-grade education and one decent arm could do to make a living. I felt very limited. Then I thought, "Well, people always thought I had a nice personality. I bet I can sell. You don't have to be very smart to be a salesperson.' So, I thought, 'I'll sell houses, that should be fun.' Six weeks later I had a real estate license and a job. I even negotiated $600 a month draw until I made a commission. That was more than I had ever made.

My very first month in the business, I had five sales. I assumed everybody does that since I was certainly nothing special. Then, my officemate, Mac, said, "Wow, Carole, you're a superstar. You made $5000 in one month. Only about 10% of the industry earns that much." That ended the draw, and allowed me and Heidi to get our own apartment.

Then, all hell broke loose. I felt like I was having a nervous breakdown. I was depressed and couldn't think. I started drinking in excess again. My life was completely out of control. In the next 11 months, I only earned $1000, bringing me right back to what I earned on minimum wage. I ended up homeless. Thankfully, various friends and colleagues took us in, so we didn't have to sleep on a park bench. I blamed my failure on my broker and lack of training,

The real story

If lack of training, or the wrong broker were the problem, why was I so successful the first month? The truth is, Eve was not comfortable with success. She wanted me to conform to my low expectations. I became paralyzed with fear. Of what, I didn't know. I was just a wreck and couldn't make a sale. I had reached my financial ceiling and hit, what is called the 'panic point'. You'll learn all about this.

<u>Husband #5 The love of my life</u>

I changed companies and got training. Most of all I read 'Think and Grow Rich' by Napoleon Hill, followed by many other books about how our thoughts dictate our lives. Within 6 months I had four transactions ready to close in one month. Once again, Glinda was on the verge of being a top producer. Heidi and I had just moved into a little apartment. I was sleeping on a mattress on the floor, but we loved it.

I was 29, statuesque, blonde and pretty, and had my broker's license. I looked like I had it altogether when I met Roy. He was 46, short, Japanese, and rich, or so I thought. He drove a new canary yellow Corvette, wore a 3-carat diamond ring on one hand and a jade surrounded by diamonds on the other. He owned his own company. Our first Christmas, he gave me a ring with 10 diamonds and 9 rubies. I thought I had hit the jackpot this time. He made me feel special. We fell madly in love. He even bought me a small condo. After one year of wining and dining, trips and gifts, we decided to get married and have a baby, his first, my third. My dream of being June Cleaver was finally coming true. I had never been happier or more contented in my life. What I didn't know, was that, since Roy had never had any children with his wife, in name only, of 20 years (who had refused to divorce him), or his two long term mistresses, he thought he shot blanks. Surprise! After 12 years on the pill, I got pregnant the very first month.

Then, Roy sat me down and dropped the bomb. He threw his W-2 year-end income statement at me, and said, "Here, read it!". I was blown away when I read that he had only made $11,000 that year, as an employee of the company, barely over minimum wage. How could that be? He confessed that he didn't own the company, but, drove a truck for them. The money he had spent that year on our lavish lifestyle, came from an inheritance. And, it was all gone. I felt so betrayed. And, livid! Here I was pregnant, expecting to be taken care of, and instead I had to get back to work. I was devastated. But, I loved him and he was a wonderful man. I forgave him and he moved in. He filed for divorce. His mother was furious! How could he bring shame on the family? His wife wanted to raise the baby. Roy stood his ground and his mother disowned him. It broke his heart that she never saw his only child. Obviously, she was as manipulative as my previous mother-in-law. I'm sure it wasn't the first time she threatened to withhold her love from Roy. No wonder he had abandonment issues.

We were happy, and I was busy nesting- papering the nursery and preparing meals. I figured I'd go back to work after the baby was born. Then, when I was 6 ½ months pregnant, Linda, the Vice President of a small real estate franchise, offered me a job recruiting and training new agents. I didn't have a clue how to teach anything, but Linda said, "Carole, you've served on the education committee for two years, and I know you've been to every seminar that came to town. You probably have a drawer full of notes and outlines. Just put something together." She was right. I was a seminar junkie and had earned my broker's license at 29. Roy believed in me and he encouraged me to give it a try. In two weeks, I had typed and cut and pasted an outline. My first class was just awful. I leaned on a desk in an 8x10 room, smoking and, mostly reading my notes. I started with 6 new licensees. At the end of the two-week class, only two were left. But to my amazement, both became very successful Realtors. And, one was the top producing agent on the entire real estate board her very first year.

Teaching turned out to be my passion. I loved it and I was good at it. (Well, after I joined Toastmasters and took a class on teaching methodology.) Glinda was in top form. My income was based upon overrides for the agents that I trained. My first month I earned a whopping $300. It took a year before I was finally having a decent month. In fact, it was more than decent, I was about to earn $6000. Once again that fear and panic arose in me. Eve surfaced and sabotaged me. I left the job, for no good reason, and never even collected the $6000. You might say money was my kryptonite.

Meanwhile, Roy had got a real estate license and started working under my broker's license. His career took off like gang-busters. Using the contacts from his previous job, he started selling land and commercial buildings. He was a brilliant man and soon he was making $200,000/year. He was confident and self-assured. This was Roy's 'higher self' shining through.

But, Roy also had an alter-ego. Let's call him Bill. Bill was almost an opposite, and he showed up early. Bill was insecure, negative and depressed. Friends and family often commented on how grouchy he was. I knew I was a good cook, but he complained about every meal I cooked. Finally, I realized, that although the entire year we dated, we had dined out in American restaurants, he only liked Asian food. I did not. It was another betrayal. He started going out to eat almost every night and took Tiffany with him from the time she was one. In addition, he couldn't get along with Heidi, who was an out-of-control teen, smoking pot, sneaking out at night, and cutting school. There was constant strife. I had to make a choice, raise another fatherless child or let 16-year-old Heidi could move out. More heartbreak. I was determined to make this relationship work, so, after we lived together two years, I finally married Roy. We paid Heidi's rent and, to her credit, she got her GED, earned her AA and is very successful.

We bought a luxury home in the foothills with an in-law-apartment and hired a nanny/cook, who I immediately sent for Japanese and Chinese cooking lessons. This pleased Roy and we now had dinner together. Roy's higher self was in control. So was mine. I was self-actualizing.

Life was good. I opened my own real estate training school. In four months, I was already starting to show a healthy profit. My old boss offered me a $10,000 sign-on bonus to return to his company as his exclusive trainer. I did, and I never collected the $10k. Never even asked for it. Once again, I was starting at zero income. Can you believe it? When I built-up my overrides again, I left the company to accept a position at a large franchise for $300,000 a year. Not bad for a high school dropout, right? Glinda was dominating once again. But Eve panicked again, and got me fired in 12 weeks.

It was the early 80s and real estate interest rates soared to 24%. Roy's sales plummeted, and he changed. Now, his default personality was Bill, his negative, lower-self. He put me down constantly. He told me my success had been a fluke. I was a fraud, a nobody. My listing in the 'World's Who's Who of Women' was a joke. I moved out, then back a several times. I couldn't stay away.

I was unemployed, but, no worries, I was on to my next adventure. I knew that the reason my proteges were some of the highest producers in the real estate industry was not because I taught them how to write a better contract or some secret skill. It was because I made them believe they could do it. I had a real gift for inspiring people. I wanted to use this talent. I was invited to present my first personal development workshop for the real estate board.

In the beginning, Roy had been my biggest fan. He attended my events and cheered me on. But, this time he refused to attend. My workshop was a resounding success. I got a standing ovation from 500 Realtors. This was the woman I was meant to be. I was bouncing off the moon when I walked in our front door to share my triumph. Wham! Roy slammed me against the wall, and shoved a .45 under my gullet, screaming like a madman, "I'm going to blow your f----ken head off, you f- - - king c-word!" Three-year-old Tiffany was watching in horror. I can feel the terror in my body just repeating the story. The nanny pulled him off me and I ran down the street screaming like a banshee. The swat team surrounded the house and Roy threw out the gun. That was the end of it. If that happened now, he would be arrested, but not in 1981. Eve took control of my life again.

For almost five years I floundered. I tried Mary Kay, and other MLMs, but after a rousing start, I tanked again and again. I left Roy several times but couldn't make it on my own. I had lost all confidence and inside, I believed Roy was right, I was a fraud. I ended up couch surfing again, this time with 8-year-old Tiffany in tow. I was lonely, depressed and spending nights in bars looking for the next Mr. Cleaver. I was miserable with Roy and miserable without him. I wanted my life back. I asked him, 'If I'm so terrible, why did you ever love me?' His reply, "Because you used to be sweet." I believed that too. I wasn't lovable.

Roy's higher self was attractive and wonderful. He just couldn't believe it. To him, I was a trophy wife. His belief was that only wealthy white men got women like me. While his career skyrocketed, he felt worthy. But now, he was living in constant fear of me leaving him. The more I bloomed, the more insecure he got. When he lost his confidence, he would either walk 10 paces ahead of me or behind me. The fear engulfed him and I guess, you'd say, he was temporarily insane when he pulled the gun on me. It was downhill from there. He wanted to get it over with, so, he kept finding more devastating ways to hurt me. He just wasn't the kind, generous and caring man I had fallen in love with. He denied me every kindness and made me start to feel worthless. It was easy to believe him. I tried one more time.

In 1987, during a brief reconciliation, I decided to give real estate sales another try. Honestly, I wasn't sure I could do it. I joined an office where no one knew me so they wouldn't have high expectations. To my surprise, Glinda took over and I became a top producer the first year. Eve even allowed me to earn $50,000. That put me in the top 10% of the industry again. Roy was still pushing me away. I was confident that I could now support myself so, I finally moved out once and for all, and got a divorce. I bought a luxury condo for Tiff (now 10-years-old) and myself and life was looking good. Glinda felt unstoppable. Until… I had $20,000 in commissions ready to close in one month. Bham! I felt like I was having a nervous breakdown. Escrows started falling apart. I made stupid mistakes. I couldn't sell a damn thing. I went into foreclosure and bankruptcy. I was flat broke. Eve flourished in those days. I felt worthless and hopeless. I hit rock bottom again. Heidi, who was now divorced with a child of her own, took us in. You can imagine the victim story I had about how Roy had betrayed me. I also had a great story about why I was failing so miserably in my business. About the time I was ready to close the $20,000, we had the Loma Prieto Earthquake. I actually thought my panic and nervous breakdown was Post Traumatic Stress Syndrome form the earthquake. I believed it.

The real story

So, what was the real story? Well, in the beginning Roy was my idol. I had him on a pedestal. He felt confident and lovable. But, over time, I started finding his faults, and pointed them out. Since his self-esteem was already pathetically low, my criticism only convinced him he wasn't good enough for me, so he had to get rid of me before I dumped him. We all need approval and acceptance and

Roy needed more than most of us. He never remarried, or even had a relationship. We remained best friends until he died with me by his side twenty years later. And, of course, my breakdown was just me hitting the panic point again.

The Alcoholic Gigolo

I was 45 when I went into foreclosure. I was a mess. For the next two years. I couldn't hold a job, or find a new man. I was very depressed and desperate to be rescued. I got involved with an alcoholic, womanizing, gigolo who had just moved here from Chicago. When Heidi fell in love and evicted me and Tiff, (who I had joint custody of), I rented an 8x10 bedroom from my sister and, stupidly, moved the Gigolo in with me. I barely knew him. My family couldn't stand him. In fact, my sister used to watch America's Most Wanted' looking for his face. LOL. I couldn't help it. If you've been there, stop beating yourself up. You did what you had to do- acted consistent with your low self-expectations.

"I deeply and completely love and accept myself."

Having a man in my life, any man, allowed me to concentrate on earning money again. I created an opportunity managing and remodeling an apartment building. I was to receive a bonus of $40,000 for the increased rents. I never got in writing. How many ways can a gal sabotage herself?

I hired my contractor friend, John, to do some major repairs. He and the gigolo hit it off and the three of us started hanging around together. I had known John for 25 years when he was dating my girlfriend, Kathy, who he later married. In fact, John and Kathy stood up for us when I married Chuck, my fourth husband. Sadly, Kathy and John had a toxic relationship. They hated each other and should've divorced but stayed together for financial reasons. Two years after John started hanging around with Gigolo and me, Kathy's breast cancer came out of remission and metastasized. She passed away in six weeks. Gigolo and I started looking for a nice woman for John. He was a sweetheart, and, owned a home.

<u>Husband #6- The Perfect Man- for me!</u>

One night, Gigolo passed out after dinner, as usual, and John and I sat and talked, and, talked, until morning. We commiserated about our lost dreams. Kathy had never supported his passion to be a remodeling contractor and he was struggling just to make a living. We talked about what it would've been like if we had been together. What could we have accomplished if we had someone who believed in us? I admired John and believed in him. John said he was a hopeless alcoholic and would not be good for me. I told him, the alcohol abuse was a habit, not an addiction. Fortunately, I was right. We have had our challenges with excessive drinking over the years, but we conquered it. He had always been attracted to me and dreamed of having a woman like me, smart, capable, faithful. Ha-ha, he hadn't met Eve. Every time I connected with him and Kathy over the years I was Glinda. I decided to give it a try. It couldn't be worse than what I had. I told Gigolo over his eggs and he cried. Not because he was so in love with me, but, because he needed me. I was his meal ticket.

It was easy to fall in love with John. I even realized how handsome my 6'2" Italian Stallion is. As one girlfriend commented, "Definitely, movie star quality." Three weeks later, John asked, "What would you say if I asked you to marry me?" I answered, 'I'd say you're crazy. Why would you want to marry a five-time loser like me?' His reply, "Because I'm going to make you happy." And, he has! I moved in 3 weeks later. That was scary! The truth is, he fell in love with Glinda. He wanted me to be the kick-ass business woman. He doesn't feel intimidated one bit.

John believes in me. He respects and admires me. Perhaps, more than I do myself. I live up to his expectations, and, visa-versa. John is not the same man who was married to Kathy. I saw great things in him. I told his adult kids that John was not the loser their mother had made him out to be and I was going to prove it. He had a contractor's license and I had my broker's license. We founded a Mom and Pop Handyman company. In three years, it morphed into a Million Dollar Design and Build firm doing high-end remodels and additions. In 1995, one year after we decided to give it a try, we married. We were both 50. He is a model husband and we are good parents to our 6 adult children and loving grandparents to 13 grandchildren. His kids love the man I brought out. They respect him now. That is a miracle to John. Kathy, in her bitterness, had poisoned the kids. And, John, feeling like a loser, acted consistent with their views of him. Now, he acts consistent with my higher opinion of him. Glinda has eclipsed Eve and I am happy and content. John also brings out my softer side, which is nice. Our families are glad we found each other at 49 years old. So, ladies don't give up.

I enjoyed the challenge and the success. I was President of NARI-SV (National Association Remodeling Industry- Silicon Valley). We were respected and successful. We won many design awards for projects I designed, and he built. Success felt really great!

However, being a remodeling contractor was John's dream, not mine. I left the firm in 2007 to pursue my own dream of being a motivational speaker. began my NLP training and became a Master Practitioner of Neuro-linguistic Programming and a Certified Wealthy Mind Trainer. I developed and presented workshops. Although, once again, I excelled at the skill, and my clients were getting awesome transformations, I wasn't making any money. This was particularly frustrating, since I was teaching people how to get over their own money issues. It made me feel like a fraud, which in turn, exacerbated the problem. I feared that Eve was surfacing again and sabotaging me. Looking back, maybe starting a coaching career in the depth of the recession of 2008 was not great timing. Anyway, after dumping about $150k, that we could ill afford, into this venture, John was becoming quite opposed to me continuing. It was jeopardizing our marriage, so I decided it was time for a break.

Besides, John needed me to take on the management of his new venture, subdividing our property into 3 lots. Our home was on one lot and I designed homes for the other two lots to sell, got the bids, set-up a website, and put them on the market. Luckily, a builder came along and bought the lots for $1,100,000 so we didn't have to build the homes. It felt good to have a million dollars' income in one year.

And that is the real story of John and me. He adores me and spoils me like Daddy did Mommy. He even cooks, shops and cleans house. He's perfect for me. Maybe I will never love him the way I still love Roy, but I am in love. Although, he is smart enough not to admit it, I think Kathy was the love of his life. And, that's okay. We have a wonderful life.

Now, I am finally, completing this book. It went smooth until I decided to include this chapter. You've probably heard of 'journaling'. I never quite understood how powerful the process is, until I started writing my story. Every time I reviewed what I wrote, I thought, 'Well, that's not quite true', and it changed. And, each time the story changed, I evolved.

TRANSFORMATION EXPLORATION 10:

It's your turn to start uncovering misconceptions about yourself. It's time to learn 'why' you have behaved in such a way to get yourself in the exact position you are in today. It's time to discover what a lovable person you really are. It starts right here, right now, with your 'story'. Writing it by hand is the best way to get all your neurology involved. But, honestly, for me, the computer was advantageous since my story changed daily. Start with birth. 'I was born with deformed arm, therefore, I had to have some man take care of me.' You might say, "I was born on the wrong side of town; therefore, I didn't stand a chance to rise above my station in life." Most of us think there were certain circumstances that made us who we are today. It's good to bring those beliefs to the surface. A month from now, you may see it differently. Now, I can say, 'Having a handicap made me more tenacious.' It wasn't my arm that limited me, so much as the expectations my parents set for me, because of my arm. Expectations, that I believed.

No one is going to see your story so just let it flow. Don't worry about spelling or grammar or rambling. The important thing is to get it out and watch it evolve. You are well on your way to success, whatever that means for you. In the next chapter, you will begin to define success and learn four keys that are essential to succeeding at anything, be it marriage, speed reading or business success.

SUMMARY:

Using the ideas, information and exercises in this book, combined with authoring your auto-biography, works. I'm living proof. Changing unconscious beliefs, and even, some conscious ones, takes work. But, it is so worth it. Only then, will you be able to be your very best, authentic self and claim the woman you were meant to be... And, you have all the tools you'll need, right here, plus your journal.

PART IV: YOU MUST ACT CONSISTENT

Do you know the story of the Scorpion and the Frog? A scorpion asks a frog to carry him across a river. The frog hesitates, afraid of being stung, but the scorpion argues that if it did so, they would both drown. Considering this, the frog agrees, but midway across the river the scorpion does indeed sting the frog, dooming them both. When the frog asks the scorpion, "Why?", the scorpion replies, "That is what a scorpion does."

It's impossible not to act consistent with our unconscious beliefs. You can logically know something to be true but act as if it isn't. That's because we must be congruent with our self-concept. Not to be puts us in chaos. It just doesn't feel right, and we have to adjust. When I was on the verge of making more money than a college grad, I felt like a fraud. My unconscious mind was shouting, "This isn't right! You've got a 9th grade education. You're too dumb to earn big money. Stop this act right now before anyone finds out!" and I would sabotage my success. This happened every time I was about to be paid more money than I subconsciously believed I deserved, given my education and handicap. I had lots of evidence of my success; awards, a wall full of certificates and plaques, and of course, the listing in 'Who's Who'. Still, inside I felt like a fraud.

Roy believed he was unlovable. He was living in constant fear of me leaving him. The more I bloomed, the more insecure he got. The fear engulfed him and nothing I did could convince him I loved him. He began to act more and more 'unlovable'. He treated me like shit and just kept finding more devastating ways to hurt me. Until, finally, I had no choice but to leave him. Twenty years later, at our weekly lunch, he said, "See, I knew you were going to leave me. That's why I refused to make you happy." Dumbstruck, I asked, "Did you hear what you just said?" He changed the subject. You see, he had to make himself right. He had to prove he was unlovable.

He never had another relationship and went to his grave loving a woman he wouldn't let himself have. That's how our self-fulfilling prophecies play out.

The good news is, often our self-concept is not who we really are. Roy was lovable. If only he could have believed it, maybe we would've lived happily ever after. I earned my success and acclaim. If only I could've believed it, I could have achieved even more and would not have been homeless. What could you achieve if you let go of a limiting belief or 'self-expectation'?

TRANSFORMATION EXPLORATION 11: FIND ONE LIMITING BELIEF

Write out one belief you hold to be true and how you act upon that belief.

PART V: ROLE MODELS

My role models in the 50's were: June Cleaver (Leave it to Beaver Mom), the mom on 'Father Knows Best' (now, there's a real clue to a woman's' stature in the 50's), and all the other sitcom women, plus, my own mother, aunts and grandmothers. All of them were homemakers. All of them were subservient. All of them were happy and contented. This is who I thought I was meant to be.

My other TV role model was Eve Arden in her role as "Our Miss Brooks", the old maid school teacher. Part of me, the authentic part, wanted to be a teacher, but then I would have to forego marriage and children. You couldn't have both. And, I knew I couldn't be Annie Oakley. Other females on TV were single gals just working until they could find husbands. There were no news anchors, not even a weather girl. The only African American woman on TV was Beulah, the lovable, wise maid. How sad was that? (Of course, it didn't affect Oprah- born in 1954). Beulah's male counterparts were Amos and Andy. For many middle-class white Americans that was how we formed, or changed, our representation of African Americans. Most middle-class neighborhoods were still segregated in the fifties, so those role models helped define our beliefs.

Fathers were the bread winners and the decision makers. They managed the money. Our household was typical. Mom didn't have to worry her pretty little head about finances. Women were taken care of. Women gave away their power to men. They signed purchase agreements, deeds and other legal documents without even reading them. After all, they probably wouldn't understand them anyway. (Surprisingly, when my father died, leaving Mom penniless at 62 years old, my mother was forced to make financial decisions. She made shrewd investments and retired in comfort and security.)

It didn't matter that even as a child, I was a leader, forming my own club, taking initiative. That was not encouraged. In fact, my self-reliance was discouraged because it was not a girly quality. I was artistic and could have been a dress designer or interior decorator, but that was never even suggested. My sisters and I were supposed to finish high school and marry, period. Obviously, when my parents decided I should get married at 14, the diploma wasn't even important. Middle-class boys were supposed to graduate high school and get jobs. They were not encouraged to be athletes, entrepreneurs or inventors. That was for pipe-dreamers.

In 1959 a new woman came on the movie scene, interior designer, Jan Morrow, played by Doris Day, in Pillow Talk. Jan had the most glamourous life. She had an exciting career and dressed like a movie star. She was also adorable when she got tipsy. Actually, she got down right drunk and had to be carried out of the nightclub. But, she still looked adorable. (A representation that I wish I had never formed!) The movie ends when she gets married and presumably becomes a homemaker. Hmm, happily ever after. I don't think I had ever heard of divorce when I was a kid.

My three daughters were raised from the 60's through the 80's (Tiffany is 15 years younger than Heidi). For Heidi life was portrayed with 60's favorite 'Gilligan's Island'. Can you sing the theme song even now? How about those women as role models? Mrs. Howell was wealthy, arrogant, snobbish and aloof. Would you want to grow up to be like her? Or, perhaps, Ginger, the sex goddess who was not too bright? Finally, there was the down-to-earth Maryanne. Was there a role model in "I Dream of Jeanie"? Yes, she was sexy, dumber than dirt, and there to please her master.

But there were positive role models in 'The Munsters and the 'Beverly Hillbillies'. Yeah, right. Then, in 1966 a career girl appeared on TV, 'That Girl' starring Marlo Thomas. She portrays a struggling actress and model. She has a career, but no husband, but she is engaged. In the popular sitcom, 'My Three Sons', about a single father of three, storylines centered on the family's adventures in suburbia, and was perhaps the hybrid of what was to become the era of the Dom-Com (Domestic Sitcom). Steve Douglas also spent a good deal of time fending off attractive women who wanted to marry him and take over that lovable ready-made family. Other 60s shows include: 'Bewitched', 'The Honeymooners', 'Green Acres'. 'The Addams Family', and 'Petticoat Junction'. Do you relate to any of the above?

In the 70's sitcoms were still showing strong family themes with the women still primarily homemakers. There's the popular 'Happy Days' and 'All in the Family' (remember Archie Bunker, the ignorant but lovable bigot?), the 'Partridge Family', and 'The Brady Bunch'. All had 'stay-at-home Moms. Heidi admits she wanted to be Marsha Brady and have her parents. (What? Instead of living with me and a step-father who beat me almost daily?) We also saw more single working girls in 'Three's Company' and 'Lavern and Shirley' (now there are some great role models!) But, a new woman also appeared on the scene. Mary Tyler Moore played a career gal in a man's world, but again, she was single. Waiting to be rescued? When I first became a career woman in the early seventies, I was given a book on 'Dressing for Success for Women'. The rule was to *not* look like a woman. We were advised to wear a conservative dark blue suit with a basic white blouse and black pumps. And, by all means, don't carry a purse or people won't take you seriously. A real estate career was acceptable for a woman because houses were a woman's' domain. That, of course was ridiculous because selling real estate is a business' just like selling stock.

Those were the role models Oprah grew up with. It is amazing that she was able to form a self-image that allowed her to become the powerful, accomplished woman she is. But, she had a savvy grandma who gave her very different expectations and possibilities. And now, you have a savvy aunt!

In the 80s TV really changed. Women commonly had careers and families. The era of the Super Woman emerged. "I can bring home the bacon, cook it and serve it with a smile, help the kids with homework, even after a hard day at the office, and never break a sweat or lose my sweet disposition." In what used to be my favorite (pre-Cosby's fall from grace), 'The Cosby Show', he was a doctor and the wife/mother was an attorney. 'Family Ties' was about Hippies turned suburbanites trying to raise a family in the narcissistic ‹80s. Mom was a Realtor®. "Growing Pains' was about the misadventures of a family with a home business father and a journalist mother. One of my favorite role models was Angela, on "Who's the Boss". She was sophisticated, successful and confident, and had a dynamite wardrobe. She was financially savvy and independent, and her house-boy, Tony Danza, was a real hunk.

The eighties also saw the Valley Girl craze. You remember, the girls talked like they had a mouth full of marbles and created their own language. Their motto, "Shop 'til you drop." Madonna's "I'm a Material Girl' described the culture perfectly. Were you a Valley Girl?

Then, there were the legendary primetime soaps, 'Dallas' and 'Dynasty'. I loved the glamour and glitz. Roy and I were Carrington wannabes. We had the big house in the foothills, diamonds and furs, a live-in nanny/maid and luxury cars. Crystal was everything I wanted to be. She was beautiful, poised, confident, and had real class. Not to mention the million-dollar wardrobe. Roy and I even assumed the haughty, egotistical air of our rich role models. At the time, that was our representation of rich people. Diahann Carroll played Dominque Deveraux, an intelligent, sophisticated African American business woman. Now, there was a positive role model. I used to imagine, visualize and affirm that I was just like Crystal (Dynasty), and Angela (Who's the Boss?) 'I am poised and confident, just like her. I am an intelligent business woman.' I began to look and act the part, at least on the surface. But of course, the 80's didn't last and neither did my lavish lifestyle of the rich and famous. By 1990 I was a has-been divorcee and Roy was living in a rental.

In the late 80's -early 90's the 'Designing Women' TV series was popular. Outspoken feminist Julia Sugarbaker ran a design firm out of her Atlanta home, along with her shallow ex-beauty queen sister. We begin to see females as more capable career women. In 'Kate and Allie', Allie Lowell divorces her husband and gets custody of their two children, she moves to New York City and moves in with her best friend. Both are working women. That was another first.

The nineties were altogether different, with shows like 'Friends', which follows the lives of six 20-something friends living in Manhattan, and 'Murphy brown', the misadventures of a tough female television journalist and her friends. In 'Home Improvement'

Jill is a domineering wife and career woman. Ellen Morgan ('Ellen') is a neurotic bookstore owner who deals with life through comedy and extensive rambling. It became acceptable, and desirable to have a career and a family. It was also acceptable to be single. That was a big change from the 50's.

So, our TV role models were one avenue that set our expectations. What we were supposed to be and how we are supposed to act. For most of us our real-life models were the same. If you were middle-class you probably didn't have rich friends that were college bound. If you lived in the ghetto you didn't see many successful entrepreneurs, unless they were drug dealers. The role models that influenced us most were from our childhood, mostly before the age of eight. It established in our minds, what is possible and realistic. That's why, in 2016, many African American actors like Will and Jada Smith boycotted the Oscars. They want black children to see someone who looks like them on that podium, so they know that it is possible for them to be great actors. It worked. In 2017 six black actors were nominated. Viola Davis won the best supporting actress at the Golden Globe Awards.

Now, here it is 2017, and women are not just weather girls, but are news broadcasters. Several CEOs of major corporations are females. We almost had a woman President. Yes, we have come a long way from the 1500s when a father would give his 4-year-old daughter in marriage to a stranger to enhance his political and financial position. Our life and happiness meant nothing. We were merely pawns to be used by men. Millions of women in third world countries still are. Count your blessings. It could be worse, a lot worse.

There are so many opportunities for women today. We truly can become anything we want to be. Many young women demand equal rights in their marriages. Men must do their share of housekeeping and child care. Maid services have sprung up like crazy. We are even fighting for men to have family leave. Women have come to understand how fulfilling a career can be. If they are fortunate enough to stay home while the kids are very young, they look forward to returning to work.

At the Vancouver Peace Summit in 2009 the Dalai Lama said, "The world will be saved by the western woman." That's you! You do have a mission. Be all that you were meant to be, and you can change the world. Does that sound too grandiose? If you change one life, and they change two, and they change two more- well you can see the ripple effect it has. You are powerful. Believe it!

The other, even more powerful, thing that set our limits is what we were told we could expect. But let's finish this first.

TRANSFORMATION EXPLORATION 12: YOUR TV ROLE MODELS

Thinking of your TV role models who did you relate to?
What representations did you form as a result?
How does that influence who you are today?

PART VI: WHO'S YOUR TRIBE

CHOOSE YOUR COMPANIONS CAREFULLY

Who are the people you spend most of your time with, and how are they affecting your abundance? Whether we succeed, or don't, is significantly impacted by our interactions with everyone in our circle. Successful women know it takes a supportive community to reach the next level, so, they surround themselves with people who cheer them on, women who are positive role models. You become who you associate with, then you attract more of the same. Hang around with the bottom of the pack, and that's where you'll stay. Collaborate with women on the rise, and you will rise with them.

Commiserating

Commiserating is a socially accepted form of complaining. We all do it, to some extent. We commiserate because we want to feel better about our own circumstances. It's like salve for our lack of success. I've done it myself. "Let's just all agree that no coaches are making money right now. There's too much competition. This is the coaching capital of the world; how can anyone make it here?" While that may have been true for the women I was commiserating with, it was not true for a different group of coaches who were successful. Maybe, in some convoluted way, we think we are helping the other moaners by sharing our own failure. "Gee, I'm a failure too." Maybe, we just want to fit in. Little did I know I was poisoning my mind and theirs.

Rather than helping your colleagues, commiserating simply reinforces a failure attitude. It makes the complainers feel helpless and hopeless. "Why keep on trying, when no one can make money in this market? Next time you're tempted to join in the negative conversation, gently remind yourself of the damage you are doing. Use that energy to talk about dreams instead. Perhaps to encourage instead of agreeing with the negativity.

Naysayers

Now, there are some negative thinkers you may not be able to avoid. These wet blankets are lurking in every corner, waiting to slay your dreams. They are the pessimists, and purveyors of doom and gloom. We call them 'Naysayers'. Often, they are people you can't disassociate with, like your spouse. Let's face it, most people don't believe it is possible to be anything other than ordinary. Friends and family, in an attempt to protect you from hurt and disappointment, may discourage you. When you are already doubting yourself, that's like pouring gasoline on a burning fire.

We all have naysayers in our lives. In fact, most of the people in our lives are naysayers. Maybe it's your mother who's called every day since you left corporate America for entrepreneurism, to tell you to get a job. Even if she avoids the topic, what energy is being created? There are several reasons that they discourage us.

1. Love- Often our loved ones don't believe it is possible to go beyond being 'average'. They have positive intentions and only want what is best for us. They want us to get *realistic*. Doubters may say things like, "Oh, get off your high-horse. Things are bad. We're in a recession." It's their duty to bring us back to sanity. I believe it is our default way of thinking. One day, John's daughter called and told me she had just bought into Mary Kay. I had tried it myself and failed so my first impulse was, 'Oh No! You'll never make it. Do you know how few women ever succeed in Mary Kay?' I was shocked that, I, the great motivator, would think such negative things. Fortunately, I came to my senses and congratulated and encouraged her instead of being the Naysayer.

2. Envy- You are going out there and you are going to make your dreams come true. There are people in your life that have too much fear to do it. Fear drives envy. Mostly, because if you are going for it, why shouldn't they? This makes them feel unsafe. They almost want you to fail so they don't have to feel like losers.

3. Fear- Roy, (husband 5), was afraid that if I became all that I was meant to be, I would leave him behind; I would cease to see him as my hero. Sadly, that became a self-fulfilling

prophesy when he constantly ripped my self-esteem and confidence to shreds.

Your Prince may also be overtaken by fear for another reason. In the beginning, you're investing more money than you are making. People who are not entrepreneurs don't understand that sometimes it takes a few years to figure it out. The investment can be a stretch on the family finances. You may have to put the Hawaiian vacation on hold for a while. (You'd do this for him, wouldn't you?) You must be strong when faced with his ire. If you don't comply, a spouse can make life hell. They'll call you selfish. John (#6) used to angrily protest, "You are trying to bankrupt us!" Which, of course was ludicrous. I was not *trying* to ruin us, I was trying to make my break through. When your loved one threatens or belittles you for following your dream, it's emotional terrorism.

If you have a Naysayer spouse, tell him, "I'm sorry you don't understand. You'll have to trust me; I know what I'm doing." Okay, maybe you're not positive you know what you're doing. But, if you have a burning desire to achieve the dream, you will never be happy without it. You will find the way. I'm not saying that you should ignore his concerns. You could lose something more precious than your career, your marriage. You may need to find a compromise. You may need to find another way to fund your dream. Always stayed tuned in to your values and priorities.

Don't understand- This is the biggest group. You'll find this is especially prevalent in the older generation. It used to be called 'depression era thinking' but it can apply to anyone who grew up with financial struggles. They seek safety and security and can't understand why you are taking such huge risk. They think we are flakey.

How to handle Naysayers.

1. Don't hang around the water cooler with the Naysayers
2. If they capture you, tell them, "Thank you for the information." Change the subject, or better yet, walk away. They will poison your attitude.
3. Set healthy boundaries- when you exercise the word 'no' you make the yes more valuable.
4. If the Naysayer is your spouse, try to enroll his help by saying, "This doesn't work for me. I am committed to my success. I accept that you are not in my corner, and that's okay. But I need to ask you for one favor. "Could you please stop raining on my parade? It's hard enough to fight my own doubts and fears without you raising more. So, could you just lay off me?"

"Surround yourself with only people who are going to lift you higher". Oprah Winfrey www.brainyquote.com/

So, those are the associates who can defeat you, where can you find like-minded women, (and, men too!) who will propel you to success?

Mastermind Groups

Andrew Carnegie was a big proponent of a form of collaboration, that he called the 'mastermind alliance', shortened to 'mastermind group'. Mastermind groups have been around since the beginning of time. Ancient Greeks and Romans used them. Governments use them; they're called the Senate. Even Benjamin Franklin belonged to such a group, which he called a Junto. In his ground-breaking book, 'The Law of Success', Napoleon Hill clarified the strategies for the alliance. His formula was to make it, 'a structured, repeatable environment for the success of all.' Hill wrote about it again in 'Think and Grow Rich' He described it as: the 'harmonious coordination of two or more minds working to a definite end'. Commiserating is adverse masterminding. It's collaborating with naysayers, pessimist, worrywarts, and negative folks who want to feel better about themselves by supporting your failure. Too many women, either operate in isolation or gravitate to women who are struggling like themselves. The more they practice this form of business suicide, the more they attract more of the same. Like attracts like. If you find yourself in a conversation that supports your failure, excuse yourself and find another assembly of higher minded women. If you don't feel like you personally have anything to contribute to the success of others group, just listen.

"No two minds ever come together without thereby creating a third, invisible intangible force, which may be likened to a third mind [the master mind]." Napoleon Hill, Think and Grow Rich

So, what is a mastermind group exactly? I like this definition from 'The Success Alliance:

"Mastermind groups offer a combination of brainstorming, education, peer accountability and support in a group setting to sharpen your business and personal skills. A mastermind group helps you and your mastermind group members achieve success. Participants challenge each other to set powerful goals, and more importantly, to accomplish them. Through a mastermind group process, first you create a goal, then a plan to achieve it. The group helps you with creative ideas and wise decisions-making. Then, as you begin to implement your plan, you bring both success stories and problems to the group. Success stories are applauded (loudly!), and problem are solved through peer brainstorming and collective, creative thinking. The group requires commitment, confidentiality, willingness to both give and receive advice and ideas, and support each other with total honesty, respect and compassion. Mastermind group members act as catalysts for growth, devil's advocates and supportive colleagues.

This is the essence and value of mastermind groups." From <http://www.thesuccessalliance.com/what-is-a-mastermind-group/>

Female Collaborations

Professional women's groups or 'communities' fill my cup. They are a supportive assembly of women with similar high goals. In the past, I always had more male friends than female. That was because my friends were not like me. I had nothing in common with homemakers or hourly workers. Many women think females are back-stabbing, jealous bitches. If that's what you think, guess what, your RAS is going to prove it. I quickly realized that my weekend workshops were much better with just women. It allowed all of us to be more authentic and vulnerable. Mentoring or coaching groups of women become a sisterhood. Together, we lost our fear of being judged. I highly recommend you find a group in your area. Your task is to find people who not only support you as you are now, but also encourage you to claim the woman you are meant to be. Join organizations, attend seminars, invest in a mentor. Start hanging out with the kind of women you want to be, not who you have been. I know when I'm around them, I feel like I can do more. When I hear the success stories of women who struggled with confidence, just as I had, I am inspired.

Yes, in order to hang with likeminded women, you may need to let go of some friends who aren't on the same wavelength. Rest assured, creating a new community doesn't mean banishing people you love from your life, but, -and this is a big but – you can no longer abandon yourself to make everyone else happy. Instead, abandon guilt. I remember when my mother went to work. She still kept a spotless home, shopped for groceries, cooked great meals, and, starched and ironed 15 dresses and 7 men's shirts weekly. It took years for me to let go of being a super-woman. Put yourself first and it will all work out. Like they say, put the oxygen mask on yourself first. If you don't, you can't help anyone else. What do we fear?

1. Fear of leaving the tribe behind. Everyone needs to belong. We need acceptance and approval, and, since we women are relaters and communicators, we have more invested emotionally in the clan. If your clan has poverty consciousness, scarcity mentality- you learn energetically that is not okay to have abundance... am I going to be banished?
2. We may fear that our friends will think we are arrogant or conceited because we are stepping out of our collective comfort zone. You may even belittle yourself in their presence to make them feel comfortable.
3. A part of you may even feel ashamed of wanting more from life than your compadres.
4. You may fear you won't find likeminded women who will replace your tribe. The truth is, nature abhors a vacuum. What's gone will be replaced.

Women's networking groups, and there are hundreds in your area, are a form of mastermind. The best are smaller groups of women (up to 25 or subdivided into smaller teams) who have been selected through a screening process that ensures they are all on the same track. These groups are coached or mentored by someone who has mastered success in their field. These groups may be industry specific. I belonged to one for remodeling contractors across the United States- or, they may be geared towards women entrepreneurs in general. Many are divided into levels of success or segmented into sub-groups. There may be one segment for women just starting an entrepreneurial enterprise, one for those who have revenues of $500,000-$1,000,000, and one for female CEOs earning over a $1Million a year. Masterminds can cost as little as a cup of coffee at Denny's or as much as $200,000 per year. You may think that, if you could afford it, you'd want to start in the higher end group. That is not the case. First, you need to learn what the lower-level groups have to teach you.

Who do you want in your community? If you need to replace some friends in your circle, start with these four primary categories:

- o Cheerleaders
- o Mentors
- o Role models
- o Advocates

Cheerleaders are your private fan club. They recognize your potential, and believe in you. They encourage you. Cheerleaders celebrate even your smallest victories. Your closest associates should all fit into this category. They're the ones who say, "You can do this."

Mentors are people you admire and trust who have walked they path before you. They've been there, done that, can warn you of the pitfalls and, help you recover after you've made some blunder. You can share your fears and your challenges. It is usually one person, perhaps a friend or Aunt. You can also find a mentor through an organization, like SCORE. SCORE is an association of retired executives who donate their time to mentor budding entrepreneurs. SCORE is a resource partner with the U.S. Small Business Administration. Mentors say, "I understand."

Role models are women who epitomize the woman you are becoming. Their very existence provides proof that it can be done. They model how to be dynamic without sacrificing femininity. They're the women who say, or imply, "You can do it, too; let me show you how."

Advocates may be on the perimeter of your associations, but they are nonetheless valuable. These are women who go out of their way to help other women. They may have a referral, an idea, a job lead, or some information that can advance your career. You may already know some. Mostly you meet them through networking. They are the ones ask, "How can I help?"

TRANSFORMATION EXPLORATION 13: IT'S YOUR TRIBE

1. If you could waive a realistic magic wand, who in your life would you spend less time with?
2. Who would you spend more time with?
3. Who are the people in your life who are:
   - Cheerleaders
   - Mentors
   - Role models
   - Advocates
4. How do you feel about doing this exercise?
5. Which list is the longest?
6. Shortest?
7. What does that tell you?
8. How did the naysayers affect you?
9. What would you like to do about them? (i.e. Love them, try to avoid sharing my dreams with them)
10. Where will you go to meet new people?
11. Keep this list handy, referred to often, keep adding new names, and have frequent contact with those in the first four categories.

SUMMARY:

This was a huge section. That's because getting to know yourself is a huge task. I hope you're not in overwhelm. If so, take heart, your brain will get accustomed to all the new data. The next subject, 'Let Your Values Guide Your Life', has had an immeasurable impact on my life. I only wish I had learned it decades sooner.

LET YOUR VALUES
GUIDE YOUR LIFE

PART I: WHAT ARE VALUES

Honoring your values is paramount to claiming the woman you are meant to be. When I first took the quiz below, I wasn't even sure what values were. I thought they were morals, like don't steal or cheat on your wife. That's part of it. You might say values are your principles or standards of behavior; your judgment of what is important in life. They represent the qualities that define you. Most of us don't consciously think about our values when making a decision or, realize how they affect our behavior, but values are always influencing us, even if only on a subconscious level.

Our values are not always obvious. You may not even know what many of yours are, or in what order. And, the order is important when making life decisions. Your personal values (should) determine your priorities. When deciding what path to follow, who to marry, where to live, how to behave- your values should be your guide. When you understand your values, you'll understand why you prefer to do what you do. And why you are drawn to certain people. You may also see why you are in disharmony with someone with whom you are in a relationship.

When your actions and behavior match your values, we call it integrity. When you live in integrity you are living your best life, you're living in alignment with your values, and you are usually content. You feel harmony in your life. You feel passionate and energetic and optimistic. The opposite is also true, if you are out-of-alignment with your values, you may suffer from burnout, depression, fatigue and confusion. Sound familiar? Yes, it is the same thing that happens when you are not being your authentic self. So, this is another piece to the puzzle of finding out who you really are.

When you say, you are an honest person, and that is a high value for you, yet you cheat on your taxes, you are out-of-integrity. You feel guilt and shame and disharmony. Does that sound conducive to success or happiness? Of course not. If you value having a husband who adores you, but you are living with one who makes you feel like dirt, you are not in alignment. It's more than the abuse that is making you feel depressed; it is the inner struggle to get in sync with your true values. If your top value is family, but you work 60 hours a week, you are out of sync. And if you don't value competition, and you work in a highly competitive sales environment, are you likely to be satisfied with your job? Does that make sense?

In fact, your values may be sabotaging your success right now. That's because your values must be congruent with your goal. When I first took the test below I had 'success, achievement and earning money' at the top of my list. My top priority goals were material. By the time I had completed it, I realized I valued my husband and my marriage more than my career. Actually, I was quite surprised. And, I sure hadn't been behaving as if that was my priority. I had invested about $150,000 that we could ill-afford in my coaching business. I had yet to make more than $1000 in a *year*. I just couldn't find what was blocking my success. John had been patient, but he could no longer support my dream. He had become a real 'Naysayer'. I felt constant stress as I fought his negativity and it inflamed my own self-doubt. Still, I doggedly pursued my passion against his wishes. When I would hire an expensive coach, he would go through the roof! I was determined to make it so, I went behind his back and then felt guilt and shame. I had never lied to him. Honesty and integrity are my highest values, even before career and marriage. I was betraying my own principles and I was in turmoil.

Then, there was the other part of me that wanted to follow my passion, felt *compelled* to follow it, and I believed wholeheartedly that if I just didn't give up I would find the way. After all, that is what my personal development books and gurus were telling me. I was, and am, a positive thinker by nature, borderline Pollyanna. I also felt extreme urgency to make it since I was already in my 60s. Can you see the inner conflict? Fortunately, I realized how much I valued my marriage and that John was no longer happy. One of my tenets in life is to never assume that my spouse won't leave me for someone who treats him better. I sure didn't want to look for number seven at 63 years old. My two life goals: maintaining a happy marriage and being successful following my passion, were in direct opposition.

So, what do you think John's top value was (and is)? Financial security. He had reason to be insecure about our finances. John had been injured on a job and was on permanent disability. That, plus me leaving the company, coupled with the sagging economy, was the end of the remodeling company. I was putting him in a state of terror. He wanted me to be happy, but he was in a panic. Being an optimist (or Pollyanna- lol) I always assumed I'd have my breakthrough in time to save us, so I didn't worry. Can you see that I was violating John's highest value?

Sadly, I realized that I had done this with Roy (husband #5) twenty-five years earlier during the 1980 crash. We had been living a luxurious life when real estate interest rates hit 24% and both of our careers tanked. I was sure that if we just thought positive everything would be alright. Roy did not. I couldn't see any reason to give up the maid. I went into Mary Kay and let my leaders talked me into investing more and more money even though I was not making a profit. The rallies were so exciting that I believed I would become a millionaire in no time. Roy called me a Pollyanna (there's that name again!) and put me down constantly. He begged me to stop spending so much money and I called him 'Mr. Negative'. I really took 'Positive Thinking' to the extreme. Roy was 17 years older than me and he was scared. I thought both Roy and John were just negative, and I wasn't going there. Now, I wonder if I had been more of a team player with Roy, if my marriage would have worked. Of course, there were bigger issues with Roy, but I was not helping to soothe his fears.

Knowing what is important to your spouse/partner is critical to happiness, yours and his/hers. There are basically 6 human needs that dominate our lives. They can change at various stages of life based upon what you value at that moment. They are:

1. Certainty- This is the need to be comfortable and avoid pain. John's number one need is to know he will always have his home and enough to eat. Roy's need for certainty was financial but, also included being 'certain' I would never leave him. Certainty was never high on my list of values. That made it hard for me to fulfill their needs.

2. Variety- To have stimulus, change and surprise in your life. It is the need to feel a variety of emotions every day, joy, awe, curiosity. This is high on my list. This is the highest need for most teenagers.

3. Significance- To feel special and worthwhile. Ladies, this is huge for men! Make him feel important, build his confidence and self-esteem and he will love to be around you. Maybe this is why I had 12 proposals. When I met men I always thought they walked on water. In my 30's, I had a session with a psychic named Paula. Paula said, "I see you have a new man in your life, Carole." I smiled in acknowledgement. "He isn't what you think he is." she lamented. I was puzzled. Paula explained, "You tend to give men qualities that they don't really possess." "Oh, that's terrible!" I exclaimed. "No", said Psychic Paula, "if you didn't, you wouldn't find anyone to date." It's true, men love to be with me because I boost their egos - until I get to know them and then I see them for the mere mortals they really are, and begin to knock them off the pedestal. Luckily, even though he is not everything I thought he was in the beginning, I still see John through my Rose-colored glasses. (Forgive the pun). Actually, he is everything and more than I thought, in the ways that matter.

When Roy first started dating me, I had just moved into my own apartment after another homeless period. I was sleeping on a mattress on the floor. I had never had expensive jewelry and clothes, so I was thrilled with everything Roy bought me. He felt significant. As life went on, and we got into the personal development craze, we started having visions of grandeur. We watched 'Lifestyles of the Rich and Famous' and set goals for yachts and Rolex watches. When Roy could no longer afford them, he felt very insignificant. Thus, he didn't buy me anything, not even birthday or Christmas gifts.

You can meet the need for significance by being courageous and claiming the woman you are meant to be. Or- by having a big problem that you can solve. I felt significant when I sold the project and very insignificant and unworthy when I failed at Mary Kay. I feel significant when a man is in love with me and definitely insignificant when I had no lover. This need was so pervasive that, in between husbands, I was obsessed with finding the next one. My mother called me 'boy crazy' and then 'man crazy' as I got older. I think *crazy* is exactly what I was- out of my mind with the need for approval and acceptance, and love.

5. Connection- You can feel connected by giving love to others or by being in a harmonious relationship. Who doesn't love that feeling? I love my relationship. John is perfect for me. Because I have 'connection' taken care of, this is lower on my list of values, now. My mother was a big connector. She had friends for life and hundreds of them. She nurtured her relationships. Not me. People flow through my life. I don't even send Christmas cards.

6.Growth- The need to grow. This is a big one for me. I need to constantly grow. I want to learn all I can, be my very best and maximize my abilities. That is why I was obsessed with succeeding. I crave growth as badly as John and Roy craved certainty. What a conflict. We all crave significance and when my values and needs were not in alignment with my husbands, no one got to feel significant.

7. Contribution- This is a biggie for us women. Ask any woman why she wants success and it will always start with how many people she can help. "I want to put my grandchildren through college." "I want to help orphaned children in Uganda." In a room of hundreds of women, over and over I hear, "I want to start a foundation to serve some segment of society." Ask men why they want success and the first thing out of their mouth might be, "I want a Porsche." Being able to help women take charge of their lives is the most rewarding thing I have ever done, and I intend to spend the rest of my life doing it!

TRANSFORMATION EXPLORATION 14: MY HIGHEST NEED

So, looking at that list, which is most important to you? Which one drives the behavior of your spouse? Interesting, isn't it? If your relationship is in turmoil, this may be why. You now can change it. Ask your partner which one is their highest need and share yours. This could be a breakthrough that will change your life. It has mine, and John is ever so much in love with me again.

PART II: LEARNING VALUES

You begin establishing your values as a child. From the age of 0-7 we imprint. We can't judge so we form neurological connections. From 7-14 we model. The first people we model are our parents, then others in our environment. We model from television and movies, church and school. From 14-21 is our socialization period when we learn communication skills. Our frontal lobe has not developed, and one cannot make executive decisions. (And, I got married at 14? Good grief! What were my parents and the judge thinking?) In the beginning, we live by the values given us by other people. As adults, we get to decide if we want to keep living by those values.

Values exist, whether you recognize them or not. Life can be much easier when you acknowledge your values – and when you make plans and decisions that honor them. When you know your own values, you can use them to make decisions about how to live your life, and you can answer questions like these:

Who should I marry?
What career should I pursue?
Should I work for this person, in this environment?
Should I accept this promotion?

Should I start my own business?

Should I compromise, or be firm with my position?

Is this in conflict with my values?

Should I support his/her dream or follow mine?

So, take the time to understand the real priorities in your life, and you'll be able to determine the best direction for you and your life goals!

TRANSFORMATION EXPLORATION 15: WHAT MAKES YOU HAPPY

Think about these things:

- What's important to you?
- What do you care about?
- What and who do you want in your life?
- When do you feel happiest? Think about a time in your life when you felt particularly fulfilled. There may have been challenges, but you were on a roll. It may have been a few minutes, or hours, or days. What was important about this experience? What values were you honoring?
- What do you react negatively to? What makes you angry or frustrated? Think about one of these things. What value is being violated? What kinds of situations cause you to feel incongruent?
- When are you *not* being true to yourself?

For each of us, there are usually values that are so much a part of us, that we don't even think to put them on a list. These are often our most dearly held values. A teacher might fail to include learning, an artist might forget to write down creativity, a business owner might overlook financial success. Often these things are so much a part of who we are, that they become invisible to us.

Tip:

Values are usually fairly stable, yet they don't have strict limits or boundaries. Also, as you move through life, your values may change. For example, when you start your career, success, as measured by money and status – might be a top priority. But after you have a family, work-life balance may be what you value more.

As your definition of success changes, so do your personal values. Therefore, keeping in touch with your values is a lifelong exercise. You should continuously revisit this, especially if you start to feel unbalanced... and you can't quite figure out why.

It's also a distressing situation when your partner's values are not in alignment with yours. It will often feel like your life's energy is being sucked right out of you. And, it is! When I coach women looking for love, I ask them to give me their list of the ideal man. It is always superficial-tall, dark hair, wears suits for work, intelligent, funny. Then I tell them to throw the list away. After we define their values, they write an entire different list. Ladies, it works! If you attract a love that is in alignment with your values you are far more likely to be happy than if he is tall, dark and handsome.

As you go through the exercise below, bear in mind that values that were important in the past may not be relevant now. How would you define your values?

TRANSFORMATION EXPLORATION 16: DEFINING YOUR VALUES

Please do this exercise in order. In other words, complete Step 1 before you go to Step 2. In fact, don't even read Step 2 before you complete Step 1. Ditto with each step. You'll see why this is so important.

Step 1: List 10 people you admire. Just quickly list them before going to step 2. This can be real or fabled beings. They can be from your own life or from fiction, history or movies. It might look like this:

1. Oprah
2. Gandhi
3. My mother
4. Joan of Ark
5. Susan at work

Step 2: Next to their names list all the reasons you chose them, i.e. He is a self-made man, she is courageous, witty, outgoing. The number one woman always listed in my workshops is none other than 'Oprah'. But what is interesting is all the different reasons women give for choosing her. Is she on your list? Why? Here's mine.

- Billionaire
- Spiritual teacher/healer
- Authentic, vulnerable, transparent
- Came from adversity and poor circumstances
- Never gave up
- Is changing lives by inspiring women

Step 3: Circle the qualities or characteristics that were mentioned more than once. Notice the common denominator.

Step 4: Realize that this is a list of your values. This is who you are at the core. Do you recognize yourself?

Step 5: Identify the times when you were happiest. Find examples from both your career and personal life. This will ensure some balance in your answers.

- What were you doing?
- Were you with other people? Who?

- What other factors contributed to your happiness?

Step 6: Identify the times when you were most proud. Use examples from your career and personal life.

- Why were you proud?
- Did other people share your pride? Who?
- What other factors contributed to your feelings of pride?

Step 7: Identify the times when you were most fulfilled and satisfied. Again, use both work and personal examples.

- What need or desire was fulfilled?
- How and why did the experience give your life meaning?
- What other factors contributed to your feelings of fulfillment?

Step 8: Determine your top values, based on your experiences of happiness, pride, and fulfillment.

- Why was each experience truly important and memorable?

Use the following list of common personal values to help you get started – and aim for about 10 top values. As you work through, you may find that some of these naturally combine. For instance, if you value philanthropy, community, and generosity, you might say that service to others is one of your top values.

Accountability	Dependability	Generosity	Learning	Time alone
Achievement	Determination	Growth	Leaving a legacy	Transformation
Adventurousness	Diligence	Happiness	Leisure	Travel
Aging well	Discipline	Hard Work	Making a difference	using my talents
Altruism	Empathy	Health	Parenting	Wisdom
Ambition	Enthusiasm	Helping Society	Positivity	Sensitivity
Assertiveness	Family-oriented	Honesty	Professionalism	Serenity
Balance	Fidelity	Honor	Reliability	Spontaneity
Being the best	Fitness	Humility	Peace	Stability
Belonging	Freedom	Independence	Power	Strength
charity	Fun	Ingenuity	Respect	Structure

Commitment	Creativity	Intelligence	Responsibility	Teamwork
Commitment	Family	Intuition	Retirement	Thankfulness
Compassion	Freedom	Leadership	Security	Trustworthiness
Competitiveness	Friendship	Loyalty	Self-actualization	Truth-seeking
Contentment	Fun	Making a difference	Self-esteem	Understanding
Contribution	Generosity	Mastery	Self-discipline	Uniqueness
Creativity	God	Openness	Spirituality	Vision
Curiosity	Growth	Perfection	Success	Vitality
Decisiveness	Happiness			
	Harmony			

Step 9: Prioritize your top values

This step is probably the most difficult, because you'll have to look deep inside yourself. It's also the most important step, because, when making a decision, you'll have to choose between solutions that may satisfy different values. This is when you must know which value is more important to you.

Write down your top values, not in any particular order.

Look at the first two values and ask yourself, "If I could satisfy only one of these, which would I choose?" It might help to visualize a situation in which you would have to make that choice. For example, if you compare the values of service and stability, imagine that you must decide whether to sell your house and move to another country to do valuable foreign aid work, or keep your house and volunteer to do charity work closer to home.

Keep working through the list, by comparing each value with each other value, until your list is in the correct order.

Step 10: Reaffirm your values

Check your top-priority values, and make sure they fit with your life and your vision for yourself.

- Do these values make you feel good about yourself?
- Are you proud of your top three values?
- Would you be comfortable and proud to tell your values to people you respect and admire?
- Do these values represent things you would support, even if your choice isn't popular, and it puts you in the minority?

When you consider your values in decision making, you can be sure to keep your sense of integrity and what you know is right, and approach decisions with confidence and clarity. You'll also know that what you're doing is best for your current and future happiness and satisfaction. Making value-based choices may not always be easy. However, making a choice that you know is right is a lot less difficult in the long run.

Here's the flip side of discovering what traits you have. Although, my daughter is 99% perfect, occasionally, Heidi exhibits a behavior or trait that is not very attractive. And, I wonder where it came from. Then, I realize, 'Oh! I do that. That is me!'. It will happen, not just with family, but with strangers. Beware, when you criticize, make sure you are not the same way.

SUMMARY:

Identifying and understanding your values is a challenging and important exercise. Your personal values are a central part of who you are – and who you want to be. By becoming more aware of these important factors in your life, you can use them as a guide to make the best choice in any situation.

Some of life's decisions are really about determining what you value most. When many options seem reasonable, it's helpful and comforting to rely on your values – and use them as a strong guiding force to point you in the right direction.

Do you value yourself? In every workshop 90% of the women say they have low self-esteem or self-worth. They don't see themselves as having value. This was true of successful, affluent women as much as those struggling to find success. It boggled my mind.

PART III: LOW SELF-WORTH

Consider some of these symptoms of low self-worth and see how many apply to you.

- I blame someone else for my situation.
- I continually blame myself even if it's not my fault.
- I do whatever you want even if I don't want to.
- I hold myself back, or avoid upsetting, hurting, angering or offending someone.
- I let others demean or put me down.
- I hold grudges, or I easily angered.
- I am reluctant to set lofty goals for fear I won't attain them.
- I'm filled with big dreams but don't follow through.
- I give up at the first sign of failure and rejection.
- I'm embarrassed or scared make mistakes.
- I don't do what I say I'm going to do.
- I am unwilling to ask for what I want, often because I don't even know.
- I hear myself saying "yes, but" a lot.
- I have no control over my time.
- I really don't see I have many choices in my life.
- I'm embarrassed when complimented.

If you checked more than two, your self-esteem needs a serious boost. Even one is a red flag. However, don't be too quick to give up on yourself because you checked many on the list. Successful women also find they are not in congruence with all their values. Many suffer from low self-esteem, at times. Women who don't value themselves often take on more than their share of responsibility (and by-the-way, often carry too much weight). So, the habit of service to others and neglect of self becomes the default setting.

PART IV: CHILD ABUSE

This may not apply to you, but I am just going to touch on the subject. I am no expert on child abuse, far from it. I didn't even realize I had been sexually abused as a child until in my mid-thirties when a therapist recognized some of the symptoms. Until then it was my dirty-little secret that I had done nasty things with grown men when I was a little girl. I was bad and I carried deep shame. Since so many women have experienced some form of sexual abuse, I just want to refer you to Dr. Phil's website where I picked up this list of common consequences of childhood sexual abuse. http://drphil. com/articles/article/705/

- Damage to self-concept/self-esteem, feeling "dirty," or like "damaged goods"
- Feelings of guilt, shame, despair and anger
- Belief that sexuality/physicality is "all I have to offer"
- High risk of promiscuity, hyper-sexuality, sexual identity problems or negative sexual encounters
- High risk of teen pregnancy
- High risk of aggressive and suicidal behavior
- High risk of substance abuse and other acting out or high-risk behavior
- Post-Traumatic Stress Disorder
- Disrupted sleep patterns and nightmares
- Regression to more infantile behavior (bed-wetting, etc.)

- Problems with memory, cognition and attentiveness
- Change in appetite or eating behaviors
- Inability to trust others
- Controlling behaviors or involvement in exploitative relationships
- Powerlessness, vulnerability and avoidant responses, such as running away
- Tendency to withdraw from relationships and society
- A fear of intimacy or commitment
- Paranoia/hyper-vigilance/phobias
- Re-victimization
- Higher incidence of mental and emotional disorders, such as anxiety, depression or eating disorders

For more information, read: <u>Child Sexual Abuse Warning Signs and Resources.</u>

If you think you may be a victim or survivor, you owe it to yourself to uncover the trauma. On the other hand, I have never delved into my own. I tried to relive an event under hypnosis but apparently, my subconscious was not willing to release it. I still can't put a face on the earliest molesters and I don't really care. I can remember some from the age of 9 and up, including doctors who touched me inappropriately when I was an adult. One chiropractor inserted his finger in my vagina, by accident. When I think about it I feel dirty and sick. I feel responsible, like I should have stopped them. Well, it all goes with the territory. I have not been incapacitated by my symptoms, and fortunately for me, I don't have very many of them, so I choose not to think about it. I 'zap' the thoughts and feelings that go with them. Try it on any experience that you want to take the sting out of.

"I deeply and completely love and accept myself."

PART V: SHAME, GUILT, REMORSE

Hardly a week used to go by that something didn't trigger a shameful memory. And, BHAMM! I instantly relived the entire degrading experience- every emotion; guilt, shame, remorse, and the fear that someone else will find out and think I am the spawn of the devil. Do you ever feel shame? Of course, you do, unless you're the guy who can walk on water. So, what can you do to stop it in its track? I find four things that work like magic.

1. Stop thinking about it immediately! You may think that is impossible. We can feel out of control when an attack of guilt or shame grabs us and holds us in self-recrimination. I've learned that if I just say, "STOP thinking about it right now!" And then turn my thoughts deliberately to something pleasant, I can keep from getting depressed. In fact, I can choose to be happy instead. What's really amazing is that in the next minute I can't even recall what I was so stressed about. Try it. You'll be blown away by how much control you have over your thoughts.

2. Zap it. Have you ever had an 'Ear-bug'? That's what they call a song that keeps playing over and over in your mind until it's driving you to distraction? Next time it happens simply say, "STOP!" It's gone.

3. Repeat, "I deeply and completely love and accept myself.

Make it ridiculous. The following exercise is a variation of a couple of NLP processes. It may take more than once to completely eliminate all the emotion behind an ordeal, but it will work.

Step 1. When a negative, painful or shameful memory comes up take a moment to focus on it. In your mind run through the event like a movie.

Step 2. Now make the movie black and white and run it again.

Step 3. Run it backward in black and white. Do it again faster, and then faster.

Step 4. Run it so fast it becomes a blur like wet newsprint.

Step 5. Now, send it out in front of you, further and further, faster and faster, until it is a tiny dot on the horizon.

Step 6. Say "Zap!" and watch it disappear.

Here's another method I used for a disturbing memory of abuse from my son-in-law.

Step 1. Start the mind-movie of the event

Step 2. Make it go faster and add circus music.

Step 3. Imagine the person turns into a cartoon character (Big bad wolf? Road runner?)

Step 4. Run the movie backwards and forwards very fast until it is a blur.

Step 5. Let it shrink and disappear. Zap! It's gone.

The thought may pop up again someday, but the emotion won't be as strong. The evil memory will stop having power over you. Of course, you won't forget the event, but you will be able to think about it without the painful emotion. That's a real blessing.

SUMMARY:

What I hope I have gotten across here, is that our most essential value is how we value ourselves. As women, we tend to under-value our contributions, abilities and talents. Until a woman learns to value herself, she is not going to be of value to her employer or client or her family. Be in integrity with your soul, act consistent with your values.

It is my desire that in reading this book you will break through your barriers. That requires that click, the recognition that you really are a capable person with something valuable to offer, and you understand that even with doubt and fear – no matter how vehemently those little voices may disagree and argue with you, that you deserve to be happy, successful, and well-paid just because you're worth it.

This sums up the discussion on values and sets the stage for the next subjects, 'Healing Your Money Story' and, 'Finding Your Value -Based Purpose'. The three are inextricably linked together. It's a logical progression from recognizing your values to finding and following your wildest dreams. A huge benefit will be giving yourself permission to earn lots of money, if you want. The reason is, earning more money is associated with an enhanced sense of personal power and self-esteem

In the end, everything in our life reflects our values, whether we like it or not. We may say we value fitness but don't take care of ourselves. We value family but don't take time for them. This incongruence is eating away at your self-esteem. Start taking small steps, or big ones if you have the backbone for it, to get into integrity. You can do it.

> "We've been programmed to sacrifice everything in the name of what is good and right for everyone else. I know for sure you can't give what you don't have." Oprah Winfrey.

HEAL YOUR MONEY STORY AND INVITE ABUNDANCE

PART I: ARE YOU DEFLECTING YOUR WEALTH?

Some lucky people attract wealth. As we know, many of them get rid of it as soon as it arrives. Then, there are those of us who are smart and capable, and, even have the opportunity, but find a million ways to deflect the wealth. As you may guess, this is a subject I have studied extensively. If you need help in this area, I advise you to do the work. I know how easy it is to get distracted; as women we have too much on our plate most of the time. However, this section can change your financial life forever, and when that happens, everything gets better.

WHAT ARE YOUR CURRENT MONEY BELIEFS

Before you can change, you need to know where you are now. So, let's start this very important chapter by looking at some common traits and attitudes that could indicate that you are deflecting your wealth and success. Read the following statements and circle the ones that apply to you.

COMMON TRAITS OF WEALTH DEFLECTORS

1. I have expressed that I feel 'trapped'.
2. I often give away my services (volunteering, or working more hours than I get paid for).
3. I crave comfort and avoid change.
4. It's so hard to ask for a raise (or raise my fees) that I just don't do it.
5. I think rich people got there by stepping on little people.
6. I am generally, co-dependent.
7. I live in constant financial chaos.
8. I have no financial goals.
9. I blame someone or something else for my financial situation (IRS, ex-husband).
10. I find ways to avoid dealing with money (bartering, credit cards).
11. I tend to sabotage myself at work. This can take many forms, i.e.:
    a. I apply for jobs that I am either: under-qualified or over-qualified for, or low-paying, or
    b. I stop short of reaching goals,
    c. I change jobs a lot, or
    d. I miss days or show up late.
    e. I miss deadlines.
    f. I invent too many distractions, (phone calls, texts, cleaning my desk, etc.).
12. I work very, very hard (long hours, or several jobs) then, I crash and burn and can't do anything for days.
13. I fill my free time with endless chores and tasks.
14. I am in debt, with little savings. If I miss a week's work, I will not be able to pay rent.
15. I have no idea where my money is going.
16. I have a family history of debt and/or under achieving.
17. I am vague about my earnings (overestimate or underestimate income; see gross, not net)

18. I continually put others' needs before my own.
19. I am frequently in pain or stress around money.
20. Recognition and praise are more important for me than the money.
21. Money isn't important to me.
22. I under-charge for my services or talents.
23. I haven't raised my prices or asked for a raise in ages.
24. I think money corrupts peoples' morals.
25. I am proud of my ability to make do with little. There is nobility in being poor.
26. I often barter for my services instead of being paid.
27. I owe more on credit cards than I can pay off in six months.
28. I tend to sabotage myself with work (apply for jobs not qualify for or low-paying, stop short of reaching goals, change jobs a lot, procrastinate.)
29. I work very, very hard (long hours, several jobs) and then collapse.
30. I am in debt, with little savings, and no idea where my money is going.
31. I was raised with financial strife.
32. I tend to overestimate or underestimate my income (see gross, not net).
33. I continually put others' needs before my own.
34. I am frequently in pain or stress around money.
35. There are fights and arguments in my household around money.
36. I am confident in my ability to make money.
37. I set high goals.
38. I use a financial software or spread sheet to track expenses.
39. I have a budget and review it monthly.
40. I have at least one month's living expenses in the bank.
41. I love money and appreciate a fine lifestyle.
42. I am very optimistic about my financial future.

43. I believe there will always be enough money to meet my needs.
44. I don't worry about becoming a Bag Lady.
45. I am determined to get a what I want.
46. I am doing the work I love.
47. I have very supportive, nurturing relationships (including spouse).
48. I like and admire wealthy people.
49. I have very little consumer debt.
50. I set challenging goals for myself.
51. I see failure as a learning experience.
52. I am filled with gratitude for the success I achieve.
53. I know how to delegate and set limits.
54. I am tenacious in achieving my goals.

Some of the above statements are attitudes about wealth, others are behaviors. If you circled two or more statements 1 to 35, you're probably deflecting your wealth to some degree.If you circled four or more statements 36-54, you're likely in the upper income brackets of your profession or industry, or you should be. Stay focused on those traits.

Even if your answers were mostly in 1-35 you probably have at least a few of the traits listed in 35-54. I suggest you take this quiz again in a few months, after you have incorporated some of the exercises in this book. I'll bet you'll have many more of the positive traits.

What did you learn from this exercise?

The good news: we have the power to change any of these conditions. In this chapter, you will discover what unconscious fears and beliefs are holding you back. It will be a lot of work and well worth it. I hope you will keep re-visiting these exercises because you will go deeper every time. Make up your mind, that it is up to you to take care of your financial health and well-being,

DEVELOPING MONEY BELIEFS

I shared how we develop our beliefs, in general. That definitely applies to our beliefs about money. In the first 20 minutes of one of my workshops I explain this ice breaker exercise: "Turn to the stranger on your left, look her in the eye. When I say go, tell her how much money you earned last year, and why." You can literally feel the 'fight or flight' tension in the room. It's like people are looking for the nearest exit. Before they speak I stop them. And everyone let's out a big gasp of air.

The point is to make people aware of the fear of being judged by the amount of money we have, as if money is a measure of one's worth. It isn't just those who don't have high enough income either. Some rich people are afraid that if you knew how much money they have you will think they got it by being greedy, or unethical. That they will be judged unfavorably because of their wealth. There is shame and guilt around money, but most of all there is fear.

INHERITED BELIEFS AND EXPECTATIONS

History was my worst subject in school, but, thanks to TV documentaries, I have become a real history buff. For me, one of the most fascinating lessons of history is how our beliefs about money were formed. Going back to the Romans, centuries before Christianity, you could see how the serfs were controlled by the wealthiest citizens. Money is power. If you don't know that, look around at how our corrupt system of government favors the wealthy. They get to make all the decisions that impact our financial well-being.

When Christianity became the main religion, the popes came from the wealthiest families. These aristocrats alone, elected the Pope.

It was a position that was coveted by all. And, why not? The Pope began to get as rich as the royalty, and almost as powerful. The corruption was rampant. The financial rape of the lower classes was justified by the aristocrat's belief that they were somehow superior by birthright. They were born to be the "Ruling Class'. The nobles were raised to believe that the lower classes were inferior in many ways and were too stupid to rule themselves. They made sure no one got any uppity ideas about going out on their own. They really believed, and inherited the beliefs, that they were doing it for the good of all. If you were born a peasant, God meant you to be poor.

The Catholic Church was in cahoots with the Royalty and Aristocrats and they conspired to keep the poor ignorant. Only the privileged (i.e. wealthy) could learn how to read. After all, if knowledge got into the hands of inferior people they might think they had rights. All decisions, the ones that kept the wealth in the control of the few (meaning the church and aristocracy) were made by the few.

In the 17th century King Louis XIV believed he was chosen by God to be ruler, and then decided he was God incarnate, (as had many rulers going back to the Caesars and even the Pharaohs). The people did not question this. The belief was passed on from generation to generation unchallenged. In 18th century France, another King Louis and his bride, Marie Antoinette had wealth beyond imagination. Meanwhile the peasants and farmers were starving. It was said that one banquet at the palace of Versailles would've fed 1000 peasants. One course, a bowl of soup, cost the equivalent of $100 per person in today's money. Then, Jacques Ropier and others, began to believe that all men were equal, 'The age of enlightenment' was born. The citizens began to realize that it was not fair for a few greedy aristocrats to have so much while the rest of the populace lived in squallier. That brought about the French Revolution and the King and Queen lost their heads, literally.

But, the French revolution didn't really change things that much. I saw a documentary on the Johnson Family (of Johnson & Johnson Baby Oil, etc.). The heirs had done nothing to earn their wealth but, they felt entitled just the same. I could hardly believe my ears when the current Mr. Johnson was asked why he had so much while others starved. He said he was chosen by God to be wealthy. I'm not kidding! He actually believed that! In the docudrama 'The Men Who Built America', Andrew Carnegie, Rockefeller and J.P. Morgan had similar beliefs, that it was God's will that they be rich and powerful and that others live in poverty.

The point is, we believe things that are not true, and these beliefs go unchallenged until we learn different. Prejudice is the result of beliefs our parents held, and learned from their parents, that went unchallenged. It is not based upon fact, but we assume it is. I watched the old black and white public announcement, 'Reefer Madness' that was on TV in the early 50s, warning of the dangers of marijuana. It shows a couple who smoke a joint and go mad and kill someone in a rage, like Charles Manson's 'Helter Skelter'. That is insane. If you're stoned, you're mellow, which to me, is just the opposite of being drunk. I've smoked since I was 30 and it has not impacted my life. Yet, the government published those lies and people believed them. No wonder my mother was terrified when she discovered I smoked pot. Isn't it scary that Donald Trump says Mexicans are rapist, drug addicts and criminals? If we don't know better, we will unwillingly adopt someone else's belief and could succumb to men like Hitler, or even the American cult leader, Jim Jones, founder and leader of the Peoples Temple, who talked his followers into mass suicide. Most of us have limiting beliefs about money. "Money doesn't grow on trees." is an adage, that creates a limiting belief. "Money is the root of all evil." is definitely a limiting belief.

Right now, you have absolute beliefs in things that in the future, you will change. You can accelerate this awareness by having a desire to be awakened to the truth. Keep an open mind. My husband thinks some of my holistic practitioner colleagues are shysters, and scam artist. He's even called them witchdoctors. I must remind him that it wasn't long ago that the medical profession thought the same thing about chiropractors and acupuncturists. Now Kaiser, not only recognizes them, but refers members to acupuncturists and chiropractors. To come to think of it, there was a time when medical experts thought that bleeding a person was a cure.

HOW DO OUR MONEY FEARS MANIFEST?

An article in The Wall Street Journal pointed out that,

"The reason people get stuck is almost always an emotional reason… And they can get stuck for years… but the consequences are financial."

It's important to stress that the main reason our prosperity is blocked, is our emotions, such as fear. Remember, fear is the expectation of something bad. This is huge! I'll bet you never associated your lack of wealth with fear. Like most of us, you probably longed to win the lotto and even fantasized what you would do with the money. Yet, statistics prove that most lottery winners are broke in a very short time. And, that after about 6 months they are no happier than they were when they couldn't pay the water bill.

On the other hand, if a millionaire goes bankrupt, they soon gain their wealth back. What unconscious expectations cause them to act in such a way to go back to their old way of life?

WHAT DO YOU KNOW ABOUT FINANCES?

What do you know about finances? I remember learning how to write a check in school, but that was the extent of my financial education. And, my parents never discussed money in front of us kids. Mother said it was because they didn't want us kids to worry. That's good. But, it would've been nice to learn about budgeting.

I was raised to believe it is impolite to discuss money, politics and religion. I can understand that a discussion on political views could cause a divide between friends. Oh my, Trump sure proved that! I understand how an atheist and a Christian could think the other is ignorant. But, why is the topic of money taboo? Why do we have so many misinformed ideas and beliefs about money? We'll briefly look at the history behind the beliefs, but first, let's start uncovering more of your attitudes and behaviors around money.

Here's a powerful way to get in touch with your emotions around wealth. I want you to say the following sentence with conviction. Say it out loud with as much enthusiasm as you can muster, then be quiet and listen to your inner voice. Ready? Exclaim, "I WANT TO BE RICH!". Listen.

How did you feel? If you're like most women (and many men too) this will feel incongruent. You may hear a loud voice inside yelling, "NO! I don't really want to be rich." That's because of all the unconscious conflicts you have about money. You will do a lot of work on this. We need enough money, whatever amount that is, but must be careful not to get too much of it. How's that for creating turmoil? We have been imprinted with beliefs that set us on a path to financial success or ruin, or mediocrity.

WOMEN RELATE TO MONEY DIFFERENTLY THAN MEN

You already know, most women are not motivated by money in the same fashion as men. If I were in network marketing and wanted to recruit a male business associate, I would show him how he could have his own yacht or jet. Men say, "He who dies with the most toys, wins." Guys have very different expectations. They are expected to provide. Provide well, and display it. So, when they get money, they like status things like Ferraris and Harleys. You won't light a fire under a woman with material things. Oh, I know, we get all excited about all the material things we can win when we are a top distributor in an MLM, but that doesn't last. To motivate her, I would tell her how her stepping into her power will allow her to change the world, starting at home. I would tell her how much money she could donate.

Historically, most of the role models in business were males. But their attitude, their mindset, is totally different than women's. And so, is it any wonder that when women joined the work force and were forced to take on the masculine model, woman got burned out. The male 'wealth consciousness' is not in alignment with our feminine mind.

Go back to your values. Where was wealth on your list? I presume it is not number 1 or, even 2 or 3. However, I'll bet, financial security is high on your list. That's way different than needing to get rich. As women, we fear becoming a bag lady almost more than death. We need to feel secure to excel. That's who we are. It's in our feminine DNA. (For me to feel secure, more than financial security, I needed a man in my life, and it didn't matter if I had to support the bum.) When we have that secure feeling, or 'state', we operate at our highest level. When we are secure, we can focus our energy and attention on doing masculine achievement. Boy, does that hit home for me!

Since John and I are the same age, I assume I will be a widow someday. It's possible I will marry again, however, not very likely, even for a serial bride like me. So, I am mentally preparing to feel secure without a man. Being financially independent will make that a lot easier than when I was young and financially dependent on a man.

EQUAL BUT DIFFERENT

In the past men ruled us, enslaved us, and used us sexually, because they were bigger and stronger. As women, we do have a certain level of vulnerability. We physically can't do everything men do. And there's nothing wrong with that. Vive la différence! I love feeling protected, physically and emotionally by a man. Knowing that John would fight for my life, allows me to be vulnerable and display my softer side at home. That's what being a woman and being feminine is all about. That doesn't mean men are smarter and get to make all the decisions. I've married strong men who wanted to dominate me. That was often an irresistible force meeting an immovable object. In other words, a power-struggle. I can be quite hard-headed and stubborn when I think I am right. So, before I married John, I made him agree, that if we couldn't come to an agreement, we would allow a neutral party to arbitrate. Oddly, the arbitrator who we both respected was Roy, my 5th husband. We never formally mediated our road blocks because one of us always gave in, sooner or later. Although, on more than one occasion, at our weekly lunches, I did get Roy's advice, and take it, even though he was often on John's side. (Too bad I didn't take Roy's advice more when we were married.)

You can be soft and feminine at home and still be a tough business woman. You don't have to be a 'ball-buster' like me to be shrewd. You don't have to be manipulative like car salesmen. You have more power right now than you give yourself credit for. Just be yourself, only the highest version. I'm going to teach you how to shift your beliefs so that you can create security- and with it, peace, freedom and independence.

"MONEY ISN'T IMPORTANT TO ME."

I hear a lot of women say, "Well, I don't really care about the money". You need to stop saying that, because every time you say, 'money is not important to me' you are pushing it away. Your very words are creating resistance. Because words reflect your thoughts and beliefs. Thoughts are energy. Thoughts attract situations with the same vibration. I know, there are other things more important than money. You may even feel uncomfortable right now. If so, you really need this chapter. Yeah, I'd rather have good health, a loving family, all that stuff. The problem is, we seem of think wealth is incompatible with the 'important' things. The two are not mutually exclusive. News Flash! You can be rich and exceedingly happy. So, my dear niece, you need to stop saying, "Money isn't important to me." People who say that usually don't have any and don't expect to get any, or, they have more than enough, but inherited it, or, they are afraid of it.

Money is important! Not because it buys Lamborghinis or yachts, but, because it determines every aspect of our life. It determines the quality of the food we eat. Wouldn't you agree that fresh, organically grown veggies and non-GMO meat are pricey? Money determines the quality of medical care we receive, and ultimately, could determine how long we live. Without money, you may have to work three jobs or scrub other people's toilets instead of following your passion. Without enough money, a woman may be forced to stay in an abusive relationship. That's pretty important, isn't it? Money determines the quality of education you and your children receive. My five-year-old granddaughter Caitlyn, is fortunate to attend the best private school in San Diego. In first grade, she was already learning violin, dancing, and Chinese. Her academic skills are far above public-school grade level. Don't you think this gives her an advantage in life? So, money is important.

When you make money important, you respect it. You take care of it, because you value it. Thus, you have more of it. If you did not think classy shoes were important, you sure wouldn't have 10 pairs of Italian heels in your closet. If you don't see the value of education, you won't make the sacrifices necessary to further your own, or your children's education. My 16-year-old grandson told me he sees no point to learning math and science. Therefore, he gets very poor grades in those subjects. I hope I motivated him to change that belief. If he understands the value, he will get better grades. If you don't value money, you won't have enough.

Now you know, ignoring money issues won't make them go away. To the contrary, give it attention. Stop ignoring it and you'll attract more. Acknowledge that money is important. Don't obsess over it, but do learn to manage it. It doesn't matter how much you make, if you don't tend to it, like you would a garden, it will not grow. In fact, it will wither and die. A woman who earns $100k a year and can't pay her cell phone bill is no better off than the woman who lives on $30k and must worry about the electric being turned off. In fact, my friend and her husband have a household income of less than $2,000 a month and they are comfortable. She even has $1,000 in the bank. That's more than many high-income women have. It is her beliefs that make the difference.

THE TWO MOST IMPORTANT THINGS MONEY ALLOWS WOMEN ARE:

<u>Give and gift</u> – I often hear women say her first reason for wanting financial abundance was to have the ability to give it away. Who among us does not want to help their family? Think about that for

a moment. Who would you be able to help if you had more money than you needed to live a comfortable lifestyle? I'll bet you didn't have to think a moment without five people popping up. What charities would you love to generously support? Wouldn't that feel extraordinary? It is in our genetic makeup.

Security. We women are afraid that we will live in poverty in old age. And sadly, since we never learn how to take care of money, that is a real possibility. According to a study done by National Women's Law Center (NWLC) released in 2017, women's poverty rates were once again higher than poverty rates for men. It also showed that:

- More than one in eight women 18 and older, more than 16 million, lived in poverty in 2016. Compared to one in nine men.
- Women made up nearly two-thirds of the elderly poor.
- More than one in three female headed families with children were poor in 2016, compared to only 17.3% of male-headed households and 6.6% of married couple families. It was even higher for Black women who were head of households (38.8%0 and Latinas who head families (40.8%)

I've coached many women who were afraid that if they had money, they would mismanage it and lose it all. You wouldn't believe how common that subconscious fear is. When you finish this course, you should enroll in a financial literacy course.

The main point here is that, it is likely you will be a single woman at some point in your life either widowed or divorced. Even if you're in a relationship, you better know what's going on. Don't fall into the trap of believing that men are better at finances. They are not! And, ignorance and trust can be dangerous, I know women who have had their husbands leave them after 35 years, and hide all the assets, leaving them destitute. My mother let Daddy handle the finances and he kept her in the dark. She didn't need to worry her pretty little head over money. He also kept them broke. When widowed at 62, mother showed her financial savvy and accumulated over $140,000- from nothing. And, she was a high school graduate.

Women should enroll in an on-line course on money management. Watch Suzie Orman. Remember, the odds are, like it or not, you will likely oversee your finances at some point. It doesn't matter how much you earn, with proper management, you can have financial security. [1]

<u>If Money Were Your Significant Other,</u>

Think about this, if money were your significant other, what would be the state of your relationship?

- In counseling
- Heading for divorce
- On your Honeymoon

Finances are a major cause of marital strife and ultimately, divorce. Financial problems can cause major illnesses, even death. There are free counseling programs available. I know, you're too busy, too tired, you don't have the time. Well, look at your priorities. Review your values. Finances impact every area of your life.

TRANSFORMATION EXPLORATION 17: WRITE YOUR MONEY AUTOBIOGRAPHY

Where are you right now with your finances? What's your payoff for financial strife? Talk to the part of you that feels out of control with your finances. Writing about this in your own journal is essential.

For example:" My financial chaos makes me feel alive. I like living on the edge." "I'm known for my ability to survive crisis. That's who I am, a survivor!" Or, "People feel sorry for me and ..."

TRANSFORMATION EXPLORATION 18: <u>EARLIEST MEMORY OF MONEY.</u>

Relax, take a deep breath, and let your mind wander back to your childhood, to your earliest memory of money. Taking time. Don't force or censor anything. Just observe whatever pops up. When a memory emerges, take a good look.

- What are you doing?
- Who else is there?
- What exactly is going on?
- How are you feeling?
- Now freeze that memory into a snapshot.
- Open your eyes and write your observations in your Journal.
- Example:

    It's Christmas eve. I'm in the car with my family watching Daddy leave the packages on the doorstep. I feel so excited, giddy. I am full of joy that we are so fortunate that we can share our presents and my old bike, with this family who had a fire destroy their Christmas. I feel good about myself. Proud of the high person that I am. Not doing it for praise because those people will never know where it came from.

<u>Answer the following questions:</u>
- Were you given an allowance growing up? Did you have to earn it?
- Did you work at a young age? Paper route, babysitting? How did it make you feel?

- How old were you when you first started earning your money?
- What's the most you've ever made in a period of time?
- What's the least you've ever made?
- What did you do with the money?
- What is your earliest experience of money?
- What are the circumstances of your financial life?
- What are the reasons you tell yourself that you have been in that position or circumstance?
- What's your payoff for financial strife? Talk to the part of you that feels out of control with your finances. Writing about this in your own journal is essential.

For example:" My financial chaos makes me feel alive. I like living on the edge." "I'm known for my ability to survive crisis. That's who I am, a survivor!" Or, "I get a lot of sympathy for my financial woes."

MODELS OF FINANCIAL STRIFE

Now let's see if you recognize yourself in any of these models of financial strife. Perhaps, you'll see a little of you in more than one.

1. The Magician, 'Now you see it, now you don't'

This was Roy. He flashed his wealth like a neon sign. He carried a $1,000 in hundred-dollar bills, wore a 3-carat diamond ring, and spent a fortune on clothes. (All of which I should have recognized as red flags!) And, he attracted wealth. The problem was, money was kryptonite to him. He would get rid of it as soon as it came. We had no savings, no property, except our home, which I had to beg him to buy. Despite my urging, we had no tax-saving strategies. Money was thrown at consumer goods to show off.

After we divorced Roy sold our home. He quickly blew the proceeds and ended up renting for the same amount as the old house payment. It was crazy. He just kept making bad financial decisions. That house is now worth well over $2Mil, and we owed just $200,000. One year he made over $600,000, (sadly, after I divorced him). Did he buy real estate? NO. Did he see a financial planner? NO. Five years later he died penniless. Worse yet, he had $40,000 in consumer debt and didn't even own the clothes on his back.

To Roy, it was always circumstances beyond his control that created his financial chaos. Mostly, Roy blamed his misfortune on others. He believed other people were out to screw him and he attracted those people. He saw himself as a victim. The truth is, it was his internal beliefs about money that brought on his financial problems. It was his overwhelming need for approval and acceptance, which he thought wealth would bring him, that had him following pipe-dreams, scams and swindlers. Mostly, it was his fear of money that was his financial downfall. He used to say the inheritance was "blood money". Money brought unhappiness and pain. He had to get rid of it as soon as it appeared.

Roy's father, an abusive alcoholic, had immigrated to the United States from Japan in the early 1900's. His mother was a mail-order bride. Somehow, his father managed to buy a small piece of land and the family farmed it and sold what they grew. It was a very unhappy childhood. While I loved Christmas, Roy hated it. Santa never came to their house. He and his eight siblings were lucky if they got a pair of shoes that had to last them all year. He was teased about his ragged clothes. You can see why he thought you must have money to get approval and acceptance. So, on the one hand, he desperately needed it. On the other, he resented it. Even in later years, when we were just friends, he boasted to me that he was part owner of some of the gigantic commercial deals he worked on. He wasn't. The 'Magicians' may express their beliefs like:

- Money causes misery.
- Money flies out the window.
- Money makes people do bad things, so you need to get rid of it.
- You should avoid money because it causes pain.
- Money determines a person's worth and I am not worthy, so I can't have it.

2. The Struggler

The Struggler lives paycheck to paycheck, struggling to make ends meet, going from one financial crisis to another, racking up debt, working incessantly with no end in sight. This even applies to those who are making, what sounds like good money. My client Lynette, 54, had struggled with finances all her adult life. She made good money as a paralegal, yet she was about $400 short every month. She was under constant stress trying to keep her car from being repossessed or the PG&E from being turned off. She got a $400 a month raise and for a few months her finances stabilized. But, soon she had a financial setback (the car broke down, or was damaged), and she was back into the financial survival mode. She got a second job and made enough money to repair the car and with the extra money she was getting on top of things. But, she couldn't keep up the grueling pace of two jobs plus a two-hour commute. She took in a boarder for $400 a month. That should have solved the problem, right? Yeah, for about three months. Then the furnace went out. Honestly, I have never seen anyone who had so many setbacks. Every time she would start to get on her feet, something would happen-car accidents, broken bones, and illness - even cancer. I think every mechanical device she owned - from dishwashers to laptops-has broken down.

Lynette used to lament about the black cloud hanging over her head. It certainly looked like rotten luck and that there was nothing that she could have done to change this. Trying to rob Peter to pay Paul catches up with you. Sooner or later, usually sooner, checks start to bounce. Once you are in the cycle of bounced check fees and bad credit, it just keeps getting worse. Lynette was so discouraged.

She agreed that she had made some bad decisions that contributed to her financial chaos. There is unequivocal evidence that our subconscious thoughts can create self-sabotage. In her case, it showed up as carelessness, like losing her rent money when she left her purse in a public restroom at a park, or leaving jewelry out when her home was on the market. We all have these things happen occasionally, but Strugglers have more than their share.

Lynette did not create all her woes, far from it. She bought cars that were lemons, a lady ran into her and totaled one car, she had injuries and serious illnesses, and other things clearly beyond her control, that contributed to her financial chaos. However, her vibration around money, played a role. The universe is pretty amazing.

Strugglers often have no idea how much money they have and how much they owe. They have no budget and, no emergency fund. They operate by wishful thinking instead of strategizing and planning. They may have goals without any plan. Why bother when you have a black cloud hanging over you, sabotaging you at every opportunity.

Often, beneath the struggler's inability to get ahead is a gaping emotional wound stemming from childhood trauma or more recent abuse. Constant financial struggle can be an unconscious attempt to find comfort because her financial tension becomes a perfect diversion from personal pain. But of course, as with all distractions, financial chaos never calms the soul, it only adds to the turmoil. Still, living on the edge of eviction or losing your car, keeps a woman in high emotional energy. I wonder if this is why Lynette has always had financial scarcity. She grew up in a highly-charged environment where her mother was abused, and was often under financial stress. That feeling of anxiety became addictive because it was mixed with love. She also grew up with a life of steak or beans. That unpredictable financial security also felt akin to love. There was something familiar and thus, in a convoluted way, comfortable about the strife.

Remember, we are motivated by how something will make us *feel*. I think that is partly why I wanted so desperately to hang onto Roy. I associated him with that feeling of ecstasy that I had when I was at my peak. He was an anchor to the lifestyle we had together and to my feeling good about myself. We fall in love because it *feels* so good. We donate to charity because it *feels* good. If we're lucky we follow a career because it *feels* so good. This is especially true for women. But, sometimes we are confused about what makes us feel good.

People think it's selfish to want to make a lot of money and it's certainly not something they want to think about. And yet, no one obsesses more about money than and Strugglers. Their mantra is "If I had more money, I wouldn't have to always think about it. I spend way too much time obsessing about where the money is going to come from." That is an agonizing way to live. Law of Attraction says, "Start obsessing about abundance and you will create it'. I'll teach you how to do that. The Struggler's beliefs might be verbalized like this....:
- What's the use?
- Money is hard to manage so why bother?
- I am not worthy of having money because I am bad.
- I can't manage money. I don't have what it takes.
- If I have a lot of money, I'll mess it up. So why try?
- Life is a struggle. It's impossible to get ahead.
- I do not deserve to have what I want.

3. The Evader

Most people evade success like the plague. They cling to their mediocre jobs, cherishing their 3% annual cost-of-living raise. They wouldn't dare risk losing their retirement benefits. Evaders thinks we entrepreneurs are flaky, irresponsible pipe-dreamers. They will always play it safe, and thus, they will never have extreme wealth, or poverty.

Evaders may be anti-wealth. When I asked my sister Pat about her goals she exclaimed in horror, "Well, I certainly don't want to be rich!" "You don't want to be rich?" I asked. "Why not?" She replied, "I don't know, I just don't want to be rich!" Pat's goal of not being rich was congruent with her subconscious fear of wealth and she materialized that state. I grew up thinking, consciously, that I wanted to be rich. However, my unconscious beliefs were not in alignment. The fear of wealth was omnipresent in my childhood, not so much from what my parents said, as they didn't discuss finances at all around us kids. It was bible study and television that fueled our fear.

Evaders are the most likely to say, "Money is not that important to me". And it isn't. That is not a bad thing, if you have enough of it. Some Evaders take great pride in living on a shoestring, believing there is virtue in being poor, and they criticize those who focus on their finances.

Evaders are often afraid of success as well. They're afraid of failing. They're afraid of rejection, of being judged, of people liking them or not liking them because of their money. They're afraid of the responsibility of having more money and fear they will mismanage it and end up worse off. Because of all their fears, Evaders may be more financially secure and have 401k's in place at a young age, far more often than other types. There is nothing wrong with wanting security. I wish I was more like them. However, this group will never have the highs of great achievement and recognition. They will never live without fear. That is stressful. And they will never have real abundance. They stay protected and secure in their comfort zone. There's nothing wrong with this, if, your comfort zone is providing for your lifestyle and not constant struggle. Evaders might express their beliefs about money like this....

- Money is unimportant to a good life
- Money doesn't buy happiness
- We are not supposed to have money because we are working class.
- Money doesn't buy happiness.
- We're not like them (rich people), and don't want to be.
- We are happy with what blessings we have.
- You have to sacrifice the important things in life to be rich and successful.
- You have to work too hard to be successful.

4. The Saboteur

Clearly, I was the Saboteur. Big time! While success came easily to both Roy and myself, money was challenging. Roy kept attracting bundles of money and then got rid of it like a hot potato, while I wouldn't let money in. that was surely a recipe for a failed marriage. We saboteurs can find hundreds of ways to screw up our success. Like the others, we believe we are victims of circumstance and bad luck. I blamed my lack of training, the location of the office, my broker, the economy, too much competition and, even the Loma Prieto Earthquake in 1989. Yet, others were succeeding despite the same conditions.

On several occasions, I earned money and never bothered to collect it. Remember the $10,000 bonus that I failed to ask for, the $40,000' worth of work with nothing in writing. Another time, I invested $30,000 hard cash in an opportunity, and walked away. I certainly knew better than to work without a contract. It was stupid. It was self-sabotage.

In my case, my 'panic point' was not just about money. I had a double whammy. As I said, I grew up believing that you either had a career or a husband, not both. I believed men liked women like my mother, subservient, domestic helpmates. When I was single and desperately needed a husband to make me feel whole and worthy, I couldn't succeed at anything. I was helpless and needed rescued. Of course, being a needy mess wasn't very appealing to well-adjusted men. We attract what we are- NO, we attract what we secretly think we are, not what we want, mores the pity.

My father was also a Saboteur. No matter how he tried to get rich, the Universe always knocked him on his ass. He was quite the entrepreneur and had studied "Think and Grow Rich'. He Invested in real estate and built up a decent portfolio, but lost it all (even the family home, more than once). He founded a vending machine company and built it up so he could sell it and retire. He sold it and carried the financing for the buyer. The buyer ran the business in the ground and returned it to Dad. He lost it all once again and he was now 60 years old. I believe that is what killed him. Cancer was the weapon, but despair was the attractor. He created constant financial struggle. Sound familiar? Yep, I inherited his unconscious scarcity mindset. When he died, he left Mom penniless at 62-years-old.

I can see why my father had limiting beliefs about money. His father died when he was about eight years old, leaving his non-English speaking, illiterate, German immigrant mother widowed with three children. She took in laundry, cleaned houses and did whatever she had to do to feed her family. Dad was 13, when the Great Depression hit, and folks no longer had the luxury of hiring someone to do their chores, so Daddy had to quit school and go to work to support the family. There was constant struggle. It was in his DNA.

Contrast that to my mother who was raised upper-middle-class. Mom knew nothing about 'Thinking to Grow Rich' but she never had the fear of poverty. Why should she, she never experienced it? Her father was a pharmacist. They managed to survive the depression without much sacrifice. Mother never knew lack. Her belief was, "There is always enough." Part of me believes that, but there was also a contradiction with my belief that wealth was evil. Mom was right. After she was widowed she had plenty to live on and still gave generously to charity.

We Saboteurs often say things like…
- Having money isn't spiritual.
- It's not right to go beyond my needs.
- Rich people are greedy and selfish and I'm a good person, so I can't be rich.
- I'm too nice to be rich.
- You should put others before yourself.

5. The Quitter

Some people join network marketing companies over and over and then quit as soon as the going gets tough, which is usually as soon as they run out of friends to present the product to. Part of them wants to be an entrepreneur but a bigger part fears who they will become if they succeed. So, they quit at the first sign of resistance. They blame others for their failure; they're in the wrong up-line or didn't get the right training or the economy is bad, (sound familiar?) Then they justify their failure. Their money beliefs may be expressed as….
- I don't have what it takes to succeed.
- No one can get ahead in this economy.
- It takes too much work.
- Who needs it anyway? Not me.

COMFORT ZONE

Remember, when I earned 10 times more in one month than I had ever earned before in a year, and all hell broke loose? Well, that $6,000 a year was my income or financial ceiling at the time. Being a Top Producer didn't fit who I thought I was. Earning big money was definitely not who I thought I was. I was a high school drop out with a deformed right arm. I was meant to be a cocktail waitress or work at Ross, and that was all I was good for. That was my comfort zone. We all have one. When we exceed our comfort zone we feel nervous, and anxious, as if something bad is about to happen. That feeling grows until we want to run- the 'fight or flight syndrome'- even though we don't really know what it is. This is known as the 'panic point' and when you hit it, chaos sets in. In my case, I had a total melt down and ended up destitute. I'd wallow in the pits for months and then make a comeback, until I would hit my next panic point and crash again. Gradually, my income ceiling rose - $1,000, $3,000, then $6,000 in one month. BHAM! Chaos, meltdown, couch surfing and food stamps again. $8,000, $10,000, $20,000- bankruptcy, foreclosure and back to couch surfing and food stamps. It was exasperating. You'll learn more about the 'Panic Point' in KEY #10- Never Give UP!

Want to find your financial ceiling? Set a goal for how much you would like to earn in one year. Write it down. It can be next year or in three years. Now, close your eyes and see the dollar amount in your mind's eye. Why wasn't it three times higher? Ten times higher? That's your ceiling. Oh, I know there are some women who wrote $1Mil. If that's you, either you really know that, in which case, lucky you. Or, you are stating that because you know it is possible, in general, and therefore possible for you. That's true, of course. However, do you really, in your heart or gut, believe it. There are some lucky souls that know from the time they are child that they are meant for greatness. The rest of us mortals must discover it.

TRANSFORMATION EXPLORATION 19: FIND YOUR INCOME CEILING

Want to see? Here's an exercise that really works in minutes.

1. Relax. Read the instructions and the do it with your eyes closed.
2. Imagine you are earning $20,000 a year. Place it in front of you. See the amount.
3. Imagine you are earning $50,000 a year. Place it in front of you.
4. Imagine you are earning $100,000 a year. See it in front of you
5. Imagine you are making $200,000 a year. See it in front of you
6. Imagine you are making $300,000 a year. See it
7. $500,000. See it
8. $1,000,000. See it.

Then open your eyes. Where was the $20,000 placed? For most, it will be low. Where is the $1,000,000? For most of us it will be high, as if …out of reach. What amount was at eye level? That is your comfort zone. Was it close to the income you think you can earn in one year? Probably. Want to raise it?

1. Close your eyes again.
2. See the amount at eye level. Let's say, it's $50,000.
3. Reach out and grab the $100,000 and pull it down to eye level.

The next time you do this exercise your cap will be higher. You see, using your brain to change beliefs is really quite easy.

PART II: DEVELOPING WEALTH CONSCIOUSNESS

So far, and we are not done yet, we are working on discovering what your beliefs and expectations of financial abundance are. Let's call it your wealth consciousness. I imagine you can now see how yours is keeping you in lack. Wouldn't it be great to live with a complete absence of money worries; an awareness that there is always plenty of money to go around. People who live with true abundance never worry about having enough – they know that creating wealth and affluence is a function of their own mindset. Or, they may not even be aware of their 'mindset'.

Make no mistake about it: wealth consciousness comes first! You will not suddenly develop wealth consciousness when you become wealthy. (Remember the lottery winners). It's the other way around. You develop wealth consciousness by eliminating worry, by trusting in the universe and in your own inner resources. Once you've secured your wealth consciousness, abundance is just around the corner. Let's start delving into your beliefs about wealth. We were all raised with certain sayings about money. These are some common ones I internalized as a child. See if you can finish the sentence.

Money doesn't grow on _____
The love of money is the root of all _____
Money doesn't buy _____
Money is a necessary _____

Now, how would you interpret these if you were eight years old?

Money doesn't grow on trees. Or, as Daddy used to say, "You must think we have a money tree in the back yard." Means: Money is scare. Apples are abundant. You eat one off the tree and it produces more. Apples are limitless, eat as many as you like. In fact, if you don't eat them soon, they will rot. Money, on the other hand, is limited. It is scarce. Once you spend it, there is no more. Better "Save it for a rainy day". "A penny saved is a penny earned."

Since there is a limited supply, if you take more than your 'fair' share someone else will have to do without. To my request for a new bicycle Dad replied, "You already have a bike. There are children with no bikes." In other words, I was greedy. Greedy children are not lovable. Wow, I felt that. "I deeply and completely love and accept myself." Consequently, I have always been very generous. I asked my mother one day, 'What is my most redeeming quality?" Without hesitation she replied, "That's simple. You are very giving." That and honesty were the highest values in our family. Keep a little for yourself and share the rest. That belief worked well for my mother, but she lived very modest life.

The love of money is the root of all evil. Means: It is the desire for riches that make people do unethical, immoral, illegal things. You can't be a good person and be rich. The two are incompatible. Therefore, you are to be admired for *not* being rich. Some people believe that money will turn them into someone they don't want to become. It's easy to see why. The media doesn't report on all the millions of dollars that are donated to charity by billionaires. We see that greed corrupts. One of my fondest childhood memories of the Christmas season was lying on the carpeted floor with my little sister, watching the movie 'The Christmas Carrol". The story was about Scrooge, a greedy, miserly, businessman who everyone hated. He was the villain. Then, there was Tiny Tim's family. They were the heroes. They were working class and barely getting along, but they had the important things in life. They had love and family.

If you were an eight-year-old, what beliefs would you form from this? Greedy people are not lovable. If you are not loved as a child, what happens to you? You can be abandoned. Wow, that's pretty scary. Patty and I made unconscious decisions right then that we would not be the rich villain that no one loved.

We still see it portrayed in movies today. What about Titanic? What is happening in First Class? Rich old men have their mistresses on their arm while the wife sits dutifully at home. The heroine has to marry the cad, so she and her mother can maintain their lifestyle of the rich and famous. They are all egotistical snobs trying to one-up each other with their show of wealth. No one seems really happy, except the unsinkable Molly Brown. Molly had new money and had different beliefs about wealth. Then, in Steerage, everyone is kind and loving, and full of joy. They don't have much materially but they have the important things in life. The evil rich men even locked the gates on the lower ranking passengers, so they were trapped. Rich people are evil incarnate!

Do you remember the TV series 'Dallas'? The characters were immoral, greedy and willing to do anything to get more money. They are not very lovable, are they? It's too bad we don't hear more about people like Oprah who has donated billions to the needy. Or Madonna or Angelina and Brad who used their wealth to help the disadvantaged. Henry Ford- gave away $5 billion. Bill Gates, Steve Jobs set up foundations. Let's concentrate on how much we can give way once we have made it.

Money doesn't buy happiness. Implies what? That only poor people are happy. That if you get rich you'll end up a divorced drug addict like the movie stars in the National Inquirer? Let me say, money may not buy happiness, but it is not a criterion for unhappiness. Money allows you to be more of who you really are. If you are unethical you may find more ways to cheat people. If you are kind and generous you will find more ways to use your wealth to help the less fortunate. Which are you? Unethical or kind and generous?

Remember how the reticular activating system makes us see proof of our own expectations? My mother always saw kind, honest people because she believed people were good. Roy always found cheats and scoundrels just as he expected. And he'd say, "See, I told you so."

<u>Money is a necessary evil</u>. There it is again. It's unfortunate that we have to have that filthy, evil money in our lives. Maybe we should go back to bartering a bag of wheat for a pottery jug. But, even then, some had much better wheat crops, so they got more pottery. It's inevitable that there will always be inequality in finances. The billions of dollars donated to charity each year came from people who accumulated more than their 'fair share'. Poor people can't save anyone.

«It is easier for a camel to go through the eye of a needle than for a rich man to enter the kingdom of God»- Jesus.

OMGosh, you mean to tell me that if I get rich I will become some greedy, morally corrupt slime ball, who screws everyone? I won't be lovable and thus will be abandoned. And, I can't go to heaven? Well, no wonder we fear money. Let's dig deep and discover your unconscious fears. The following exercises are going to be emotionally exhausting. Please take time, maybe days, or even weeks to complete them. The revelations will just keep coming.

TRANSFORMATION EXPLORATION 20: EXCHANGING BELIEFS

In the first column list everything you believe about yourself and money. Put down whatever comes to mind. You can always erase something or add more to it later. Now in the second column next to each belief write a new belief, one to replace the old one. You may have some positive ones you want to keep. Great! But if the belief is getting in your way, or causing pain, find one that feels better and write it down. Here's an example:

What I believe about myself and money	What I choose to believe
Keeping money for my pleasure is selfish and greedy	My having wonderful things and experiences in my life does not take away from anyone else's opportunity to have the same thing
If I get rich, I'll be arrogant	When I am rich I am still down to earth and authentically humble and sweet
If I'm rich, I'm better than other people	I got rich because I have had some great fortune to learn something that other people didn't know, but I am no better than anyone
It's better to give than to receive	It is blessed to receive with great gratitude the abundance of the world
Being rich makes people stingy	Because I am rich I can help less fortunate people
I should give away what I don't need for my basic needs	I am a very generous and still have money left for a glamorous lifestyle for myself. I deserve a better lifestyle, just because.
Money is the root of all evil.	Hoarding it, using it to gain power for evil purposes, putting money before integrity- is evil. I use money for good.

What we focus on expands

We already know that what we think about, we bring about. Here's another important fact, 'that which we focus our attention on-expands'. If we focus on the fear of poverty, we will spend our mental energy worrying. That makes it impossible, to create great abundance. Our fear gets in the way of our creativity and traps us in the status quo. In other words, our fear "Interferes" with our means of creation. Just as my fear of abundance drove me to lose sales that I could have easily closed when the fear was quelled. A few weeks ago, I lost two valuable rings. I was obsessed with finding them. Did I leave them at a hotel? Did the maids steal them? I would wake up worrying about it. Finally, I decided to, just let go and stop worrying. I told myself, "They will show up." A few days later, voila, there they were. They had fallen between the safe and the cabinet.

If we let go of worry, if we maintain wealth consciousness, (verses a poverty consciousness) money will flow to us in inexhaustible ways. We'll literally create ways to keep money flowing in our direction. Our antennas will be on the lookout for new and exciting opportunities. And, when they appear in our minds, we will act on them. When you focus on struggle and all the things you lack in life, you just create more of the same. When you are in that state of mind, an opportunity can drop in your lap and you won't recognize it. And, your mind goes to the dark side. You look at the opportunity and see all the reasons it won't work. You see only impossibilities, road blocks, and predictions of disappointment. When you have a wealth consciousness you think, "What if...?" "What if it could work?" "What if I give it a chance?" "How could I make this work?' "What can I do to make this work?" Can you imagine how that opens the mind to see possibilities? I must admit, I deal with this all the time. My wonderful husband's default setting is, "This will never work because...." I've learned to preface my opportunities with, "John, please keep an open mind to my suggestion and let's see how it might work before you decide it will not work. Fair enough?" It's made life so much easier. When one person in a relationship is positive and the other negative it is a constant pull on the positive partner's energy. After a few years of marriage, Roy (husband #5) went to the dark side. He became depressed and very negative and angry at the world. It was sucking the life out of me. It can make you physically sick and even be life threatening. If you live with someone who is killing you with negative energy, get out if you can. If you're not in a position to leave yet, try to balance your energy by spending as much time as possible with positive people.

The other thing about abundance thinking is its ability to attract money. It's the strangest thing; when I am open to prosperity unexpected checks come in the mail, all the time- refunds on insurance premiums, refunds on an overpayment on an old mortgage, an unexpected class-action suit payment, a reminder that I had a credit remaining someplace. And, I'm not talking nickels and dimes. I've often received checks for well over $1000. John found $9,000 that he had hidden away ten years prior to our marriage. Others have attracted thousands of dollars of unanticipated funds. Open the flow of abundance and you will love the surprises.

Sometimes, even what seems impossible happens. I have been trying to close the escrow on our development for two years and ran into obstacle after obstacle. We were told we must file a Public Report from the BRE (Bureau of Real Estate). Not only is the cost prohibitive, but it will delay closing for up to a year. Meanwhile, I have a deadline on closing the escrow and on paying off money we borrowed for the project. We've spent months negotiating with the City and the BRE and got nowhere. We spoke to various attorneys and every expert we could find. It seemed hopeless.

Then, last week, I asked my sister NLP coach to see if I still had some block. I assumed when I sold the project for $1.1Mil, I had raised my income cap to that level. Not so! As Vicky guided me though an exercise I literally saw a plexiglass barrier between me and the money. She helped me to remove the barrier. I felt different. I felt open (as opposed to constricted) and optimistic. Yes, you can feel it when you have made a big breakthrough. Yesterday an attorney appeared in my life that has the solution for which we've prayed. Where was he while the plexiglass was up? Invisible to me. My RAS was only letting me meet people who confirmed my hopelessness. NLP is magic!

TRANSFORMATION EXPLORATION 21: TIMELINE THERAPY

Here is a good exercise to help you remember events or messages that imprinted your beliefs about money. In my NLP (Neuro-linguistic Programming) training we were instructed to stand on an imaginary timeline on the floor and imagine that the place we were standing was 'today' and the line behind us was our past, in front, our future. We were instructed to slowly walk backwards into the past until a memory popped up that may have had something to do with our current circumstances. I was very skeptical. In fact, I was very uncomfortable, because I was sure that nothing would happen for me. I just went along so I wouldn't look uncooperative. To my amazement, as I stepped backwards on my timeline, a strong memory surfaced. I vividly recalled an incident in my childhood that contributed to forming my opinions about wealth.

Suddenly, there I was, eight years old, sitting with my parents and my two sisters in the grand Fox Theatre in downtown San Francisco. I could vividly see the red velvet drapes that surrounded the walls two stories high. My eyes were glued to the vision of horror on the big silver screen. Without thought, I now felt a huge wave of emotion come over me. For there, in living color, on the big silver screen were the Christians in the Coliseum being fed to the lions.

And, that for me was a huge 'Ah ha! I had no idea of the representation I had formed in my mind at the time. But, somehow, now, standing on this imaginary line, it was clear to me. The Christians were the chosen people of God, the ones who would get to go to heaven. They were clad in humble, simple robes, like Jesus. In the grandstand, sat the wealthy Romans clothed in velvet and jewels. They were cruel, horrible people who would not go to heaven. Of course, my parents had no idea of the opinions and beliefs that the movie created in my eight-year-old mind. I'm convinced they had similar views. What if they had healthier beliefs about wealth themselves?

That negative imprint could've been turned around if, on the way home, Daddy would've told me and my sisters that the wealthiest people are kind and generous. And, that there is no honor in being poor. What if he had said, "Carole, when you grow up you can be as wealthy as you decide to be. And, because you are prosperous, you will be able to be generous and do a lot of good, donate to charities, and help those less fortunate. Your success will earn respect and you will have power and influence." I'm sure I would've found a way to have more to give away.

Remember my story about the 'Christmas Carroll'? We still watch that every year. Come to think of it, I never told my girls that Scrooge was not an accurate model of a wealthy man. Yes, there are Bernie Madoffs. But there are also philanthropists. Money allows you to be more of who you are.

> "Disillusionment with yourself must precede enlightenment." Vernon Howard

TRANSFORMATION EXPLORATION 22: COMPLETE THE SENTENCE

Read each of the following sentences three times completing the statement with the first word(s) that come to your mind. Write your answer down. You can make it a sentence or just a word. Don't overthink it. Let yourself go with your very first reaction. And work quickly. You can always change your responses later.

STATEMENT	FINISH STATEMENT
Example: Rich people are…	big-headed

Rich people are...   not going to heaven
Rich people are...   lucky

- Rich people are (repeat before each answer)
  o _____, _____, _____

- If I had money I'm afraid I would
  o _____, _____, _____

- My father believed money was
  o _____, _____, _____

- My mother believed money would
  o _____, _____, _____

- In my family discussions about finances were
  o _____, _____, _____

- My early experience of money was
  o _____, _____, _____

- Money equals
  o _____, _____, _____

- If I had money, my friends would
  o _____, _____, _____

- In order to have more money, I need to
  o _____, _____, _____

- When I have money, I usually
  o _____, _____, _____

- If I could afford it, I would
  - o _____, _____, _____

- Poor people are
  - o _____, _____, _____

- I would have more money if
  - o _____, _____, _____

- I've been taught that money is
  - o _____, _____, _____

What did you learn?

How did your early experiences or parental messages affect you? What would you like to change?

TRANSFORMATIONAL EXPLORATION 23: UNEARTHING MORE BELIEFS

DIRECTIONS: On a sheet of paper or in your journal, answer all the questions in both sections and then review them. You will surely be amazed at some of your beliefs.

1. What were the positive and negative events in your childhood that shaped your relationship with money?
2. What was your parents' relationship with money (your observations)?
   - "I think that my Dad's/Mom's beliefs about money were..."
   - "I think that my Dad's/Mom's beliefs about money were..."
3. The effect of their beliefs on me was:

4. Finish the sentence: "I am (am not) in the exact money situation that I'd like to be in because:

5. What do you need to do to have or make the money you want:

6. What stops you from having or making the money you want?

Whew, you burned a lot of brain cells on those exercises, didn't you? And, there's more.

About now you may be wondering when we are going to get to the changing part. But, dear niece, you are not ready yet. You see, we have only scratched the surface of your beliefs. You are going to learn so much more about yourself before you start the transforming. Be patient. Do the work. Before we leave this section, here is one more powerful exercise.

TRANSFORMATION EXPLORATION 24: 50 WAYS TO FIND THE MONEY

This subdivision has turned into a huge debacle and drained our finances. Had we known it would cost over $300,000, we never would've began. But, we made it this far and we aren't going to give up until I get that million dollars in my pocket. Meanwhile, cash-flow is challenging. Then, last week, our insurance company sent a cancellation notice on one of our rentals because the roof is worn out. No insurance, and the lender forecloses. It seemed hopeless. How could we come up with $17,000 in 30 days? Then, as always, I found a way. John and I sat down, with a pencil, paper (and a bottle of cabernet) and did this exercise. In 10 minutes, we had found the money. Here's how it works. Simply start listing all the possible ways you could make money. It does not have to be something that you would really do, just write it down. It may lead to something that will work. You are strongly urged to get to 50 ways. We only made it to 13. I had things like sell my Infiniti (NOT!), babysit for neighbors (I rarely even babysit my own grandchildren!), sell the 65" HD TV, (YIKES!) But then, out of the blue, came solutions that will cost nothing. Good, no pain.

SUMMARY:

My guess is that you learned a lot about your unconscious beliefs around money. Are they in alignment with your values? Can you see how they may be sabotaging you? Take some time now to write your own money autobiography. The past is what it is. You can't change that. What can you change then? Your representation of what that meant. Instead of, "Scrooge was not lovable because he was rich". Change your belief to "Scrooge was not lovable because he was greedy and selfish." It makes a world of difference.

YOUR VALUE BASED
PASSION AND PURPOSE

"Man's mission in life is to give birth to himself, to become what he potentially is." Eric Fromm

Just what does it mean to have passion and purpose? Well, let's first talk about purpose. One could say your purpose is best described as your 'calling or talent'. It's a call to live your divine life. What are you called to do? What is your talent or gift? It is the authentic you.

Maybe you think you don't have a divine purpose for your life, or maybe, you just haven't found it yet. It's that secret desire buried deep within your heart. That 'thing', that when you think of doing it for a living, your critical inner voice says, "Are you crazy? That's not practical, get your head out of the clouds!"

You probably had a clue when you were a little girl, as you will see. Then, you lost it, or grew out of it. That's because we learned that our dream was just a childhood fantasy that we should let go of. Our self-talk sounds like this: "Who am I to think I have something to offer the world? I'm not special. I'm not good enough. It's not practical. It's selfish." Those are all lies. Some say you wouldn't be given the dream if you couldn't achieve it.

"Your aspirations are your possibilities." Samuel Jackson

Passion, on the other hand, is not something you create. You can't do affirmations to make you feel it. You either have it or you don't. Answer these questions:

Do you ....

Look forward to getting up in the morning?
Wake up without an alarm?
Lose track of time doing your thing?
In your spare time are you reading about your career?
Or, are you working to pay your stinking bills?
In a job you're qualified for but isn't fulfilling?
Or, worse yet, a job that's sucking the life out of you.

Did you guess that 1 through 4 is what you get when you feel passionate about your occupation? 5 through 7 is what you get when you just work for a living instead of following your purpose. People who are in lackluster jobs, invented TGIF and Blue Monday. Not so for those of us who get to follow their passion.

You get up early, stay up late to do your thing. Your husband complains you work too hard. LOL, he doesn't know you're having fun. People say they don't have the discipline to be successful. They don't understand Passion & Purpose. It doesn't take willpower for an artist to paint a masterpiece. It doesn't take discipline for a trumpeter to play his horn. Tiger Woods did not have to drag himself to the golf course to practice.

I just experienced that with another one of my passions, painting. I painted a mural on 2 nine-foot doors to my master suite. Just like when I am writing a speech or book, I woke up every morning to work on my master piece, as giddy as if I were catching a plane for Disneyland. It is the best art I have ever produced. I couldn't tear myself away to cook or balance my checkbook. I barely got dressed or put on eyebrows. I was obsessed. Frankly, by the time I was finished, I was exhausted, but absolutely fulfilled. Do you know what I mean? I love looking at it every day. I feel the same way about the workshops I have created and presented. I would do it for free if I could, And, often I have, mostly unintentionally. The problem with many creative, gifted entrepreneurs is that we hate marketing and selling. That is a guaranteed formula for failure. It doesn't matter how gifted you are, you will fail big time if you don't let the world know about your magnificence.

> "Your talent is God's gift to you. What you do with
> it is you gift to God." Leo Buscaglia

In fact, your purpose could be that thing you have been doing most of your life for free! I told my friend Bonnie, "You should be a coach, you're always giving wise guidance to friends." It would have been a natural for her, but, she is happily retired from her 6-figure sales career and, her passion and purpose right now, is being a grandmother and traveling. She is very happy and contented and she is the best grandma in the world! That's a gift. I am a natural born motivator. That is my gift.

Our passion and purpose is not permanent. Like Bonnie, your focus will change over time. In Silicon Valley I see many women who are fortunate to be able to afford to stay home when the kids are young. Their purpose is parenting, to nurture and teach character, to attend little league, and, be the maid and cook. Then, when the children reach a certain age, she heads back to her 6-figure career.

> "To live our divine life, to feel fulfilled, contented, authentic, and in alignment we need to follow our life's purpose." ~Carole Rose

Sadly, many of us never discover our passion and purpose. That doesn't mean they will never have fulfilling lives. One may enjoy a career without it being the fait accompli. But clearly, it's not ideal. Remember what Mary C. Crowley said,

> "Success to me is finding something that you love to do so much, that you'd do it for free, then learning to do it so well that people will pay you well to do it."

Or not. Meaning, it doesn't have to make you rich...if you can afford to do it for love, more power to you. Remember, success is not measured by money alone. Naturally, your purpose must be in alignment with your values. That' the first thing to consider. What's important is how your work makes you feel. Do you feel valued? Are you able to contribute to the good of the company? What kind of environment do you thrive in? Is it fast paced and you are given a lot of opportunities to create or implement plans in your own vison, or do you like structure. Do you like established procedures that make you feel comfortable and secure? Is harmony an important value of yours or are you a drama queen? So, start with your values from a previous chapter and then do the exercise below to help you find your passion and divine purpose.

What happens if you don't follow your bliss? At the least, you'll feel discontented, even disconnected. Maybe, you will burn out and begin hating your life, as I did when I was following John's dream, instead of my own. Not surprisingly, all the stress and poor lifestyle led to cancer, three different kinds. I'm convinced not following my passion, almost cost me my life. And it wasn't too good on the marriage either. Make sense?

Do yourself, and your family a favor and, do what you love to do. Maybe it won't pay as well in dollars, but by Jove, you will be happier and healthier and that makes you more loving. Isn't that what life is all about? Isn't that what your loved ones really want? Go for it! You're not too old. Colonel Saunders was 65 when he changed careers. I say 65 is the new middle-age. I know, you need the stinkin' job to pay the bills. So, start visualizing your compelling future. Start talking about it, start believing that it is possible and that you deserve it. That alone will make you a happier person. And, what you focus on intently, if you congruently want it, it will materialize. It's the law!

TRANSFORMATION EXPLORATION 25: FIND YOUR BLISS

In your journal, list your favorite activities as a child. Engaging in these activities helps in awakening your authentic self. Sometimes when I see myself in the mirror wearing a classy business suit, getting ready to share my wisdom with an audience, I think my 8-year-old Carole Jo would be proud of me for breaking away from the self-expectations that had kept me in chaos.

Even a favorite childhood book can serve as a door to self-discovery. Try rereading one of your favorite books from elementary school, and I can almost guarantee that you'll have major insights about your authentic self.

What section of the book store do you gravitate to?

When you think about being of service to others through your work, were do you get the most joy?

What comes naturally to you that you love doing?

Who do you wish you were more like? This is usually a clue that you're meant to do something similar. Also, listing people whose lives you admire, as you did in the chapter on values, is another way to spot patterns that can reveal your passion

- Oprah- very spiritual-billionaire
- Spiritual teacher/healer
- Authentic, vulnerable, transparent
- Came from a disadvantaged childhood
- Never gave up
- Changing lives by inspiring women
- Allowing wealth to flow to her
- Generous

TRANSFORMATION EXPLORATION 26: MY PERFECT CAREER

Before each question put attention in heart, take a few deep breaths. Close your eyes. Don't think, just listen. After you receive an answer, open your eyes and write it down.

Who am I? (Listen, then write it down)
What do I want? (Listen, then write it down)
What will having that give me? Listen
What is even more important than that
What's even more important than that benefit
What creates joy for me? Listen
What are my unique skills and talents- Listen

Clues to your purpose can be found in your unique talents and what you simply love, and it usually will serve others in some significant way. By taking inventory of your gifts and talents you may be able to spot common themes.

What contribution do I want to make to the world? Listen

That is what ignites burning desire. When an individual is on purpose she is empowered to control the events in her daily living and will ultimately make valuable contributions to the world.

> "Success is the ability to fulfill your desires with effortless ease." Deepak Chopra

List 10 things which will make your life and your work ideal. Complete this sentence, "When my life is ideal. I am _____

> Choose your top five, and list order below

> Rate each of your top five passions on this scale of 0 to 10

> Write a paragraph on each passion, answering the question: What does that look like?

Means_____ etc.

CONGRUENCY TEST: VALUES+ PASSION= LIFE PURPOSE

SUMMARY:

Nothing can bring you more joy to earning a living than following your passion and purpose. I'm not saying you should quit your J.O.B. tomorrow to pursue your dream of being an opera singer, just because you love to sing. Even if you are gifted, it may take time and sacrifice. Keep your thoughts focused on the prize and let your RAS (reticular activating system) find the way to manifest it.

> "If we did all the things we're capable of doing, we would literally astonish ourselves." -Thomas Edison

DARE TO DREAM

"America allows more people to dream than any other place in the world. All that matters is how big you want to dream and how hard you want to work." Carly Fiorina, former CEO, Hewlett Packard and 2016 Presidential Candidate

Imagine I am giving you an all-expenses paid 2-week vacation, with a budget of $10,000. You can go anywhere you want. Your boss has already given you the time off, with pay. (Now we're really fantasizing.) The only condition is you leave in 10 days. What would you be doing for the next 9 days? Planning. You'd probably make a list of the places you want to see and things you want to do. You would then have to prioritize them. You'd want to cram as much as you possibly could into the 10 days. You would collect brochures with pictures of faraway places. You might even leave them out or pin them on the wall and look at them often, which would peak your excitement even more. You would be joyous every day just anticipating the trip. What do you think, am I right?

Now, how much time have you spent planning the rest of your life? What's your bucket list look like? Are there places you'd like to see., things you want to do or have. Have you put it in writing? A 1979 study of Harvard MBAs revealed some incredible facts about goal setting. The interviewers asked one telling question: "Have you set clear, written goals for your future and made plans to accomplish them?"

- 84% had no specific goals at all
- 13% had goals but they were not committed to paper
- 3% had clear, written goals and plans to accomplish them

In 1989, the interviewers again interviewed the graduates of that class. You can guess the results:

The 13% of the class who had goals were earning, on average, twice as much as the 84 percent who had no goals at all.

Even more staggering – the three percent who had clear, written goals were earning, on average, ten times as much as the other 97 percent put together.

(Source: from the book <u>What They Don't Teach You in the Harvard Business School</u>, *by Mark McCormack*)

> "Goals are dreams we convert to plans and take
> action to fulfill." Zig Zigler

In his autobiography, 'Be My Guest', Conrad Hilton explains, "Goals are dreams with the addition of action." That's the difference between a pipe-dreamer and a goal directed person. Pipe-dreamers have grandiose dreams, but are all talk and no action. They don't really believe for one minute that the dream is possible. Successful people have dreams and many are unrealistic, but they believe that all things are possible. That belief motivates them to take action. They make the list, even though they have no idea how to make it materialize. They imagine what it will look like when they arrive and, who will be by their side. The plan begins to materialize once they have the goal.

> "Dream lofty dreams, and as you dream, so you shall become. Your vision is the promise of what you shall one day be; your ideal is the prophecy of what you shall at last unveil." James Allen- As a Man Thinketh

So, the first thing you must do, is to decide what you want. This may sound easy, but remember, your subconscious may not think that your dream is appropriate, and it has many tricks to prevent you from achieving it. That critical inner voice will try to scare you, shame you, and even make you feel foolish. Don't listen. In fact, fight back. When that voice says, "You can't do this, just who do you think you are anyway?" You need to answer this way, "Thanks for the information. Now, shut-up!" For now, take heart, if you have desire, there is probably the will and where there is a will, there is a way. I am going to take you through a step-by-step process to set goals.

We want holistic success.

When setting goals think about these four quadrants

Business and Finances	Family and romance
Health & Longevity	Spirituality

I think these quadrants are self-explanatory so I won't belabor them. I'll admit, not all quadrants are ever in balance. Maybe, you've been working too hard and neglecting your fitness program. Maybe, your financially stable but have no romance. Maybe, you claim to be a Christian but haven't been to church since you were a kid. It's time to re-evaluate your priorities based upon the values you discovered.

When setting goals, you want to be sure they are formed in the positive. Rather than saying I don't want X, rephrase it to, 'I want' X.

Don't want	Want instead
To be fat	I want to be trim and fit
To be broke	I want to attract money and am debt free.
Have creditors chasing me	I want to feel proud that I have excellent credit. but live on a cash basis.
An abusive relationship	I want a person who treats me with respected and love

SMART GOALs. Here is a simple recipe for SMART GOALS

S- Specific. Goals must be specific. Not just, 'I want to be rich" or "I want to thin." Give the subconscious details so she can create it.

M-Measurable How much money is 'rich'? How will you know that you have succeeded?

A- Achievable. Let's face it, some things are not achievable. I'm never going to be a basketball player, no matter how much I work at it.

R- Realistic. Roger Bannister broke the 4 minute mile by seconds. He didn't set a goal to do a mile in 3 minutes.

T- Time table Give your goals a date for accomplishment. Make it realistic but not impossible.

TRANSFORMATION EXPLORATION 27: ACTIVATE YOUR DREAMS IN WRITING

This is a step-by-step formula.

STEP I: Decide what you want. Consider each area of your life. Don't worry if some overlap, just let it flow. Bring back that 8-year-old little girl who believed anything was possible. Begin making lists for every area of your life. Write them as if you already have them. Here's some ideas to get you started.

<u>Business and financial-</u>

Career Goals-
- I am following my passion and earning a good living doing _____ This is how my ideal work day looks:
- I easily rise at 6am feeling excited about starting my day.
- My office/workspace is serene with my favorite colors (name them, see it), my colorful vision board is displayed
- My work colleagues are like this _____
- Now, imagine a perfect work day. What time does it start? End?
  - o How are you dressed. Won't this be wonderful?

Financial
- I am earning $_____ doing what I love.
  - o Later you will set a 1 year, and 3 year goal
- I own my own home
- I am debt free except my home mortgage
- Imagine sitting on the balcony or patio with a glass of Merlot? What do you see?
- Feel the warmth of the fireplace on a winters eve? Think about Christmas or some other holiday you celebrate, what does your home feel like now? Feel the happiness.

- Where will you vacation?
- I am cruising down the highway on a sunny day, in my 30' motorhome
- I enjoy traveling the world first class.
- Entertainment: (example- dancing, concerts, wine tasting, etc.)
- My net worth is $_____

Family
- My children are … (example: thriving, getting good grades, fit, well-behaved, etc.)
- I am happy and proud that I have saved enough money to pay 1 year's tuition for my grandson's college education
- I am grateful that holidays at my house are full of laughter and love.

Romance- I am sharing my life with my soul mate.
- His/her values are in alignment with mine
- My love is more spiritual, than religious
- My love has a great relationship with his/her Mother. (Father, siblings, ex)
- We share the same interest in books and movies
- I love that we exercise together 4 times a week.
- My love is my best friend and we enjoy hours of just taking
- He is drug free and drinks in moderation
- He/she is financially secure
- We will plan to start a family together when after we buy a house
- We will meld his highly functional children with mine.

Health & Longevity-
- I am easily maintaining my ideal weight because I love eating healthy.
- My favorite foods are leafy, green vegetable

- I'm so grateful that we have not had a drink in three years
- We learn to cook healthy meals
- I love that I have learned how to prepare organic foods
- I enjoy exercising five days a week
- I enjoy taking my 5 min. breaks every hour to stretch or bounce or dancer or walk up and down the stairs
- My energy has never been better.
- This is how I got/stay fit. Be a little realistic here. If you hate veggies, it is not likely you will become a vegetarian.

Spiritual- What can you do to be more in alignment with your spiritual values?
- Who will you help? Charities, family, church, disadvantaged women
- How will you give back? Many women start foundations. Maybe you will support a cause.

STEP II Reverse engineer it.

After you have your list of dreams, use reverse engineering to create a plan for attaining each one. Pick one goal. As an example, we will use a career goal of being a top producer in your company. What will be the evidence that you have obtained the goal? Specify three different ways in which you will know that you've succeeded.
1. You won an award
2. You earned $50,000
3. You got a promotion

Reverse engineering goes like this:
- What was the last thing you did to reach the goal?
- What steps did you take just before that?
- Work backwards until you reach tomorrow.

So, using our example you would've.

1) How many sales or clients did it that take? Let's say- 12 -1 per month
2) What is your closing ratio? Let's presume it' 1 in 4 presentations?
3) How many presentations will you need to make to close 1 sale/ month Answer: 4
4) How many prospects do you need to contact (phone, in-person networking, etc.) before you get a presentation. You might say, "For every 20 people I tell about my product, I get one presentation. (Need 4/mo for one sale) Thus, I need to tell 80 people. 20/week
5) Create a plan to get in front 20 prospects a week. This is the most critical part of the sales cycle. And, also the hardest. Prospecting takes discipline. You might consider the following:
6) Progress- How will you know you are progressing toward the goal.
   a) What will have happened?
   b) What are some mile-stones?
   c) How will someone else know you are moving toward the goal?
   d) What does it look like, taste like, feel like?
   e) How do you feel inside?
7) Benefit—What is the ultimate benefit to you in achieving the goal? When I succeed, my reward will be:
   a) Financial freedom
   b) I will be happier and more fun to be around
   c) I will be a more positive person
   d) I will know that I have provided opportunities for my children
   e) What will achieving this goal do or get for you that is even more important? Dig deep to find the higher benefit. "I'll be more confident, less stressed."
   f) On an even deeper level what gets to happen for you. "I'll be healthier and ultimately, a better wife and mother."

g) On an even deeper level what gets to happen for you? "I'll live longer." "I'll have inner peace."

8) Qualities and abilities: What qualities, abilities, or talents do you need to achieve the goal.

a) Which ones do you already possess?

b) How will you develop the others, or find someone with the attributes you lack?

9) Downside. Define any possible downside to accomplishing your goal.

a) Who else might be impacted and how will they be affected?

b) What consequences may that have on your relationship?

c) Take the part of anyone that will be impacted. Step into the other persons shoes and think about what they will feel. Will they feel threatened? Afraid? How will they try to impede you?

d) How will others perceive and react to your accomplishment of the goal or your actions or plans to achieve the goal? Not everyone will be thrilled with your success. See "Naysayers"

10) Barriers. Identify any barrier to achieving your goals and what you plan to do to address them. Okay, get it all down on paper. Keep going. Don't be a Pollyanna and think there will be no obstacles. There will be. Make your list, then answer the following questions:

a) Have others succeeded in spite of the same obstacles? You can bet they have. Don't let obstacles be excuses. They are just bumps in the road.

b) What will I do to surmount the obstacles? You can begin thinking about this but, don't expect to have all the answers now.

c) Am I capable of manifesting this dream?

d) What could stop me from reaching the goal?

✓ My negative husband

✓ Lack of money

✓ Not enough time

    ✓ Not enough discipline
    ✓ No confidence
    ✓ Need training

  e) Is there anything you could lose or would have to drop off from your life to attain your goal?

  f) What else can prevent you from having the goal?

11) What attitudes and attributes will you need to effectively deal with these potential problems?

  a) Which do you have?

  b) Which will you develop and how?

12) Support: who will you need to support you or assist you?

  a) What capacity or purpose will they serve?

  b) Will you get a coach? If so, what would you want from a coach?

13) Actions. What exactly will you do to achieve this goal?

  a) Build an action plan or business plan. Break it down from big picture to small. i.e. You already know you need to get in front of 20 potential prospects per week. Make a list of all the possible ways you can do that.

  b) Networking

    i) Associations,

    ii) Women's groups,

    iii) Chambers of Commerce

    iv) BNI (Business Networking International) groups https://www.bni.com/ and attend weekly

  c) Present 3 free informative talks per month to target groups

  d) Make 10 cold calls per day

  e) Send 10 notes per day asking for referrals

  f) Social Media

Do this with each major goal. Then, follow the process with the life you want to manifest.

STEP III. Future pace

Imagine it is five years from now and you have done it! Really, be there. See your surroundings in great detail. Maybe you are accepting an award for top sales person. Maybe you are on a scale after dropping 100 pounds. Maybe, you are looking over the balcony of your cabin on a ship cruising own the Danube. Maybe, you're holding hands with the love of your life. Feel the joy, pride of accomplishment and the self-respect. The more detail you provide, the easier to manifest the goal. You will be doing this with each goal that is important to you.

STEP IV. Create a vision board.

I want to encourage you to start a vison board. If you haven't heard about it, here's how to create a typical one. Start with a stack of magazines and a 24x36 poster board. Cut out pictures of places you want to go and see. Things you want to do and have. Glue them to the poster. You can also write things with markers. I have one photo of a senior couple in sweats walking. I placed a head shot of John on the man and me on the slender, fit woman. I have a picture of a woman, probably in her 70s, at a podium, fit, and lovely. Now I'm in my 70s and I'm walking with Chili (Chi-Pom). John is very active with constant "honey dos" around the house. I have a sign that I wrote with a marker "$2Mil Net Worth by 2013". We tanked after the recession in 2009 and our net worth went from $1 Million to minus $500,000. But, because I had the goal, and saw it daily, my reticular activator was like radar looking for the way to make it happen. It seemed like an impossible dream. Then, I sold our lots for over a million dollars. The Law of Attraction works that way.

The goal is to look at your vision board daily and, most importantly, imagine you are already in possession of the goal. Let the Universe or God decide how it will manifest. And, for goodness sakes, don't argue with it. If the goal comes to you in an expected way, accept it with gratitude.

STEP V. 3x5 Prompt cards

Take the top 12 goals above and write them on 3x5 cards. Give them a target date.

- Post them on your makeup mirror, monitor or anywhere you will see them often.
- Read them at least 3 times each day. As you read them, imagine they are already completed. How do you feel about your accomplishment? Feel powerful.

STEP VI. Visualize.

The practice is more powerful than you can imagine. Close your eyes and envision each category of goal. Let your imagination soar.

STEP VII. Enlist Support

The best thing you can do for yourself is to find a coach and/or a mentor. Especially, if you are entrepreneurial. In addition, you will benefit from a mastermind group. The main reason my remodeling company went from $60,000/year to $1Mil/year was that I invested in a mentoring program. It may seem costly, but you will save many thousands of dollars by cutting your learning curve.

STEP VIII: Review these goals often. Re-create your vision board. Have your children create vision boards.

STEP IX: Now let's give all the goals a time frame and a 30-60-90 Day Plan of Action.

In the next 30 days I will   Completed, Extended,
                                                      Removed

GOAL	Actions I will take	C, E, R
Get accustomed to eating more leafy green vegetables	Plan a menu every Sunday Look up recipes on Foodnetwork.com Shop at Sprouts for organic veggies	
Be exercising 4X week	Search Craigslist for a treadmill Get up at 6 am to workout Join a gym Buy running shoes	
Have a complete draft of my business plan	Search web for template Hire a coach Join Score (If you are an entrepreneur this is a wonderful, and free, resource.)	
Have interviewed for 3 jobs	Update my resume Research companies that support my values. (Imagine going to an interview, and when asked why you would want to work for them, you answer, "I have researched your company and your values are in alignment with mine.")	

In the next 60 days I will

GOAL	Actions I will take	C, E, R
Be employed in my dream job	Get wardrobe ready Fix brakes on car	

In the next 90 days I will

GOAL	Actions I will take	C, E, R
Begin dating	Join a singles group at church Sign on to match.com Tell everyone what kind of life partner I am looking for	

In the next year I will

GOAL	Actions I will take	C, E, R
Have credit cards paid off	Get free financial counseling Set a budget Cut up all but one card	

You can have as many increments as you like and go as far out as you want. You may want to say in 12 years I will retire with the love of my life and $X income. Believe me, even if you don't hit it, you will be so far ahead of others who don't set goals.

STEP X. WHY

I know this is a lot of work, but it is also inspiring, fun work, so let's take goal setting a step further. As you look at each goal or set of goals (like Romance or Fitness), Ask yourself this question. WHY?

On your financial goals you would ask: Why do I want to increase my income? What would I have in my life that I don't have now? Examples:

- I want a better life for my kids
- I want to help my mother
- I want to get divorced
- I'm sick of struggling
- I know I'm worth more
- I'm scared what will happen if I don't
- I want to visit Tahiti
- I always wanted to create a foundation
- I worry about retirement

Did you notice what is wrong with many of these statements? They're phrased in the negative. Now, take your own and be sure to rephrase them in the positive. Do this with each group, i.e.,

- Why do you want a relationship?
  - o I want someone to enjoy traveling with
  - o I want help raising my children

Now ask yourself these critical questions:

- Why not?
- Why not me?
- Why not now?

Goal	Why not	Why not me	Why not now
I want someone to enjoy traveling with	There are no good men out there	The good ones don't want me	I need to lose 10 pounds first
I want someone by my side when I get old	I'm already old	I'm not pretty enough	I need to work on myself first
I want hot sex	Men are looking for younger women	I'm too fat	I'll wait until I can afford liposuction.

Nothing will happen without a plan

I taught you how to reverse engineer your action plan. It can look pretty overwhelming. Don't try to eat the whole elephant in one bite. Break your action plan down to bite size pieces. What would you like to achieve this month, week? Here is a format for a 'TO DO LIST'

Write down last Month's Commitment

Did you accomplish it? Mark which is true for you

YES! And I will celebrate by	
No- I'm rolling it over to this month	
No-I'm taking it off the list	
No-I'm delegating it to …	

This month- What is the 1 main thing you must do in each area of to get the biggest results?

Business & Finance	Write business plan
Family & Romance	Have lunch with daughter-in-law
Health & Longevity	Begin an exercise program
Spirituality	Attend church
Other	

What tasks do you need to do this week t accomplish the above?

Write Business Plan	Download various business plans and outline mine
Have lunch with daughter-in-law	Schedule the date and place. Call and set up
Begin exercising	Find buddy, join gym, buy shoes
Attend church	Arrange for babysitting, research churches in area
Other	Clean patio furniture, get teeth cleaned

Needless to say, you will also need a list for today. I put my goals for the day right on my Outlook Calendar and open it first thing in the morning. That includes exercising and necessary errands. It's easy to get distracted, especially, when you work from home. It annoys the hell out of me to see dust on my furniture or dishes in the sink, but, I *try* to ignore it and be diligent in pursuing my goal. You must make a conscious choice to stay focused. Manifesting dreams is all about our choices we make at the moment.

<u>Your Success and Gratitude Journal</u>

Don't forget to journal just before you go to sleep. The time before you fall asleep is an opportune time for your subconscious mind to work on manifesting your goals and dreams. Journaling puts you in a positive frame of mind, thereby attracting solutions to obstacles.

Include

>3 things you are grateful for or simply repeat what you wrote before
>3 things you are proud that you did today
>1 burning question that needs a solution

It takes less than five minutes and has so many benefits. After a while, your mind will automatically go to the feeling of gratitude and open a whole new world of possibilities.

TRANSFORMATIONAL EXPLORATION 28: WRITE IT, READ IT, FEEL IT, BELIEVE IT

In your journal, write this sentence. "It's time to make more money." The sheer act of writing it starts to program your unconscious.

>Read, out loud and with conviction, what you wrote
>Write this sentence: "Next year I will make $_____.
>How did you feel writing it? A little scared?
>Did you feel uncomfortable?
>Did you notice any resistance?

Do this again next month, and every month, until you have no resistance.

SUMMARY:

Planning the rest of your life takes time, doesn't it? Just keep coming back and reviewing your dreams. They are not set in stone. Revise them, set new target dates, delete them, anything goes. Do not chastise yourself for not attaining one. You probably won't achieve many of them. However, I guarantee that, even if you don't look at them for a year, you will have achieved more than you would have without the written goals. If you review them often, you will you will have accomplished even more.

You'll be amazed when you pull your list out of the drawer someday and see how many things you manifested.

"The greatest achievement was at first and for a time a dream. The oak sleeps in the acorn, the bird waits in the egg, and in the highest vision of the soul a waking angel stirs. Dreams are the seedlings of realities." James Allen 'As a Man Thinketh'

CHANGE A BELIEF ~ CHANGE YOUR LIFE

This entire book is about changing beliefs. You've done (or not) several exercises to accomplish that. In this chapter, you have the *opportunity* to do some profound processes that will help internalize the new beliefs. The more you do, the faster you will manifest your dreams. These techniques are proven to work. It's up to you.

NLP BELIEF CHANGE PROCESS

Let's begin with my favorite change process. You can use this on beliefs, goals, behaviors, even attitudes. It's powerful. Pick something you want to change and go through the process. Don't pick something too intense like, "I'm a worthless piece of shit!" Start with some small issue. I will use an example of a belief, 'I can't help being fat because I love food.'

Present State + appropriate resources = desired state

Create anchors: You can use paper to create actual space markers for anchors or you can simply imagine the different spaces in front of you.

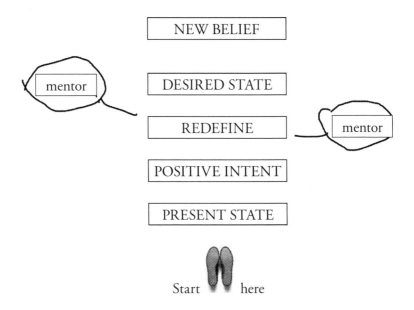

1. <u>PS (Present State)</u>: Standing in the START HERE space, select an un-resourceful belief, behavior or attitude that is limiting you, that you want to change. Gather information about the present state (in this case, a belief).

   Answer the following:
   o   Where, when and with whom does this happen?
       At home, especially when I get bored. In restaurants with friends, at parties. On holidays. Pretty much any time.
   o   What are the cues that trigger it?
       Seeing food or a picture of it, or hearing the words, 'Toll House Cookie', smelling food, boredom
   o   What can you do to make it stronger?
       Imagine taking a bite.

o   State the belief in simple, childlike language.
     "I can't help it if I'm fat because I love food."
o   Write it down. Say it out loud 5 times.
o   Where do you feel it in your body?
     "I feel my chest constricting and my breathing becomes laborious. My head lowers. My brows furrow and I feel like crying."

Step onto the PS (Present State) anchor: Notice how accurate it feels

o   Acknowledge any feelings that come up for you and breathe into them.
o   Recognize that these feelings are appropriate to the belief that you've been holding for all these years.
o   Drop inside and notice where the feelings are in your body.
o   Notice what images and thoughts the belief statement evokes in you.
o   Breathe into the feelings.
o   What is the pain that you associate with it that has kept you from taking action to change? *I don't want to feel hungry and deprived. I can't do it because I have no will power or self-discipline. I feel ashamed of my weakness.*
o   List all the pleasure you got from *not* following through on these actions. *By not sticking to my diet,*
     I get to enjoy eating anything I want.
     Food is my comfort source
     It makes me feel happy

Future pace. Look in front of you and decide where your future is, then look to the left or right of it and vividly imagine what your life will be like in 5 years if you have held onto the existing belief. See what you see, hear what you hear, feel what you feel. Add emotion. Really be in your body. Feel the pain. Make the picture even more vivid. Make it bigger and brighter. Ask yourself the following:

o   What will it cost you if you continue with the behaviors this belief creates?

> *I will keep getting more and more obese.*
> *It will affect my health.*
> *I'll probably get diabetes*
> *I will look even worse in clothing*
> *I won't be able to ever fly again, and thus miss out on seeing all things on my bucket list*
> *I won't be able to work because I'll be disabled*
> *I won't want to make love*
> *I'll look ugly*
> *The weight could eventually kill me*
> *I won't be able to walk, let alone dance*
> *I'll feel ashamed and embarrassed by my weakness*
> *My knees will fail*
> *I may have a heart attack*
> *I won't be able to care for my kids*
> *To get maximum leverage, keep this list going as long as you can*

What do you look like now? It will It helps to see it in your mind's eye.

> *I am 70 pounds heavier and can't even fit in my fat clothes anymore.*
> *My knees won't carry me, so I am in a wheelchair*
> *I have no quality of life*
> *My husband has abandoned the bed*
> *I am filled with shame*
> *My kids are embarrassed when I show up at their school*
> *I have developed diabetes*
> *I'm tired all the time*
> *I am ashamed, deeply ashamed*

> *I can't go up the stairs, so I have to sleep alone on the couch*

Imagine it's 10 years from today and you have stubbornly held onto this limiting belief. Ask yourself the same questions.

See 20 years into your future. Ask the same questions. Reach deep. Imagine the worst possible scenario.

"I will die a lonely, old, bag lady. I will probably have poor health because I can't afford insurance."

Keep going until you're crying. Then, go even deeper. Associate enough pain that you must change.

2. <u>Break state:</u> Now, shake that off. Repeat your phone number backwards. It was a false future. It doesn't have to happen. You have a chance to change your destiny. Right now!

3. <u>Positive Intent</u>: Step onto the Positive Intent Anchor. Ask yourself, "What valuable function is this performing?"
   o *"Let's me believe it is not my fault that I am fat. Therefore, I don't have to feel guilty and ashamed for being weak."*
   o What else? *"When I was slender, I got too much attention from men and it got me in trouble so being fat keeps me safe."* Whoa! What just happened here? The real problem surfaced, *fear*. If you dissect any limiting belief or behavior, it usually boils down to fear.
   Get more information on the limiting belief: What happens when I am slender?
   o *"In the past, because so many men were attracted to me, I didn't work hard enough on my relationships. I thought I could do better and I didn't appreciate the man I was*

with. It ruined my marriage and destroyed our family. I am ashamed of some of my behavior I exhibited because of that belief." (Wow! That was heavy. Is it true? I never knew that about myself. That's a good reason to stay fat. The discoveries just keep coming.)

- o What needs to be preserved? *"I want to be a loyal loving wife."*
- o And if you have _____ (what needs to be preserved) what does that get you that is even more important?

  I will make my husband happy.

- And if you have _____ (last answer) what does that get you that is even more important?

  I will have a happy marriage

- o What does having _____ (last answer) get you?

  Contentment. Satisfaction. Joy.

- o And, on an even higher level, if you have _____(last answer) what does that allow you to do, be or have?

  Security and safety. (That's pretty core. In fact, it is the second level of Maslow's hierarchy of human needs.)

- o Validate and honor the purpose and know that the positive intent, *"Security and safety."* will be still be there when you change the belief.

4. <u>Redefine</u>: Step onto the redefine anchor. In this step, you begin to loosen up the limiting belief and formulate what you want instead.

   - o Clarify the OLD limiting belief. Get it down to one sentence if possible. *"If I'm slender, I will fuck up my life."* Say it out loud about 5 times. How does it feel? *'Yeah, that feels right to me"* o   Where do you feel it in your body? *"I feel my chest constricting and my breathing becomes laborious. My head lowers. My brows furrow and I feel like crying."*

o   Why is this true for me? (evidence) *"I left five husbands because I thought I could do better. I went to bars and flirted thinking men would fall at my feet and would want to marry me."* (How embarrassing to admit. Of course, I did have some evidence of that since I had met three husbands in nightclubs.)

o   Is this always true for me? *"No, when I was happy, I didn't stray."*

o   Counter-example: Is this true for everyone? Do all slender women stray when they are not happy? *"No, of course not."*

o   Opposite: Can fat women also look for love and approval outside their marriages? *"Sure."*

Mentor 1: Step off the redefine anchor and pretend you are your mentor, someone who you imagine epitomizes the belief you want? *"Jane Fonda"*. What would Jane say to Carole about staying fat, so she will not fuck up her life?

> *"Carole, it wasn't your body that caused you to stray. It was the fact that you were in pain and wanted desperately to escape. The men you loved and trusted in the past hurt you. Being pretty just made it easier to leave. You have a husband who adores you, and you would never betray him. It's okay to be trim again. You are a good person and a loyal wife."*

o   Step back on the redefine anchor and listen to what your mentor told you. Can you accept that as truth? *"Yes, logically I know it is true now,"*

Mentor 2: Find another mentor, one that believes in you, and repeat the process. What would Roy would say?

"Carole, you were at your peak when you were 35 and a size 10. If I had made you happy you wouldn't have been in bars looking for someone to love you. It was my fault you strayed, not yours. You were faithful and loving when I gave you the love and approval you craved. The same was true of Chuck. You were desperate to escape the abuse and you needed a man to rescue you. Now you have John. John gives you the love and approval you need. You will always be true and happy with him. You are safe to be slender again. Besides, you don't use alcohol as an escape anymore."

   o   Step back onto the define space and receive this mentor's advice. Hear the words, feel what it feels like in your body. Is this true? *"Yes, absolutely!"*

   o   Is this belief, "If I'm slender I'll fuck up my life," something you would pass on to a child? *"Gads, no!"*

5. <u>DS (Desired State)</u>: Identify the desired state and create a compelling future.

What do you want instead? Create a well-formed outcome. This step is critical! It means, get a clear idea of what you want instead. Imagine for a moment what your life will be like when you have the new belief or goal. Link massive pleasure to the change.

"I want to eat healthier, drink less, and, enjoy being slender again and know that I will still be a loyal wife. I want to know that I will still be safe and secure."

   o   Where, when and with whom do I want this?

"At home, especially when I get bored. In restaurants with friends or alone, at parties. On holidays. Pretty much any time."

What gets to happen as a result of the new belief? List all the benefits you will gain by taking action or, in this case, changing the belief.

"I will think like a healthy, slender person."

"I will naturally make healthier food choices, and enjoy it."

"I will still love food and indulge in desserts and French fries, but will not eat them as often. I will be much more active and pain free."

"I will love shopping for clothing because I will look great in everything!"

"I will eat healthy snacks, or a meal every few hours and I won't feel hungry or deprived."

"I will feel like a million dollars with renewed vitality, optimism, and mental clarity."

"I will be riding my recumbent bike 30 minutes a day."

"John will tell me how gorgeous I am."

"John will be whirling me around the dance floor as we show off our waltz."

"I will meet new men and not think they are hot for my body." (At 73 years old that should be easy, lol)

"Sex will be better if I feel pretty."

"I will be a better role model for my daughters."

"I will be able to go for long walks."

And, on an even higher level, what will all that get you?

"I'll have love and a happy marriage."

And, if you had _____(last answer) what would that get you that is even more important?

"I will feel good about myself."

And, if you _____(last answer) what does that allow you to be, have, do, or become that is even more important?

"I will have more confidence."

And, if you had _____(last answer) what would that get you that is even more important?

"Contentment. Satisfaction. Joy."

And, if you have _____(last answer) what do you get that is even more important?

"I'll have security and safety." (Well, what do you know, I get the same ultimate benefit from being slender as I did from being fat.")

Put the new belief in a simple statement. *"I can be slender and fit and be the best possible me!"* (Notice, I didn't say, *"I am slender..."* That would be a lie and my subconscious would tell me so every time I repeated it. *"I can be..."* creates possibilities.)

o   Is this a belief you would teach a child? *"Absolutely!"*

Imagine what your mentor will say to you about the new belief.

How will you know you've got it?

"I will wear a size 12"

"I will be exercising daily."

"People will comment on how great I look."

6.   Future Pace: Look out onto your real future line. Imagine what your life is like in five years having changed the old limiting belief. *"If I'm slender I'll fuck up my life!"* To, *"I can be slender and fit and be the best possible me!"* Engage all your senses. See yourself (disassociated) on a screen. What do you look like? How does it feel to be the new you?

o   Take it out 10 years. See what you see, hear what you hear, feel what you feel.

o   Repeat with 20 years. Reach deep. Imagine the best possible scenario.

"I will live to 105 and be healthy and alert... I will have traveled the world because I was able to earn a lot of money."

Then, go even deeper. Associate more pleasure to the new empowering belief. Step off the anchors.

o How's your health as a result of holding this new belief?

o Who is in your life?

o Are your loved ones proud of you? See them looking at you.

o Ecology: Is there any downside to having the new belief or behavior? Does it have any negative impact on anyone else?

o What have you missed? Yes, what have you missed by changing your belief?

Associate into the new you. Step into the image on the screen and immerse yourself completely into being that better you. Breathe deep and enjoy the feeling.

7. <u>New Belief:</u> Now, holding that feeling, step onto the New Belief anchor and repeat your new statement.

"I can be slender and fit and be the best possible me!"

o Put both arms up, reach for the sky, bounce on your toes and repeat your new belief with conviction.

o Yell it!

o Get excited. Repeat it again and again.

And, state 5 things this will allow you to have, be, become, or do.

"I can be slender and fit and be the best possible me! And this allows me to:

o *wear my skinny jeans again,*

o *go sightseeing on foot*

o *feel beautiful*

o *hear John say I'm gorgeous*

o *have more energy*

Recycle through the anchors again.
- o Step onto the PS anchor and repeat the old belief. Does it feel the same? It should no longer feel true.
- o Step onto the positive intent anchor. Does the new belief honor the positive intent of the old one?
- o Step onto the redefine anchor. What do your mentors have to say about the new belief?
  - a) Look 5 years into your future. Do you like what you see now? Look 10 and 20 years ahead.
- o Step onto the new belief anchor. Repeat your new belief.

8. <u>Look at both destinies</u>: Decide which one you're committed to living, then return to the present. Keep these two valuable core beliefs in your mind at all times:
   - o The past does not equal the future
   - o There is always a way – if you're committed

"The greatest achievement in life is to have the ability to create the world around you, so that it matches the dreams in your mind." – Mike Dillard

TRANSFORMATIONAL EXPLORATION 29: EXCHANGING BELIEFS: You did this exercise with money. Now do it with other beliefs.

In the first column list everything you believe about yourself. Put down whatever comes to mind. You can always erase something or add more to it later. Now in the second column next to each belief write a new belief, one you'd like to replace the old one with. You may have some positive ones you want to keep. Great! But if the belief is getting in your way, or causing pain, find one that feels better and write it down.

What I believe about myself and money	What I choose to believe
Men don't love fat girls	The right man will love me and desire me, just the way I am.
If I get rich I'll be arrogant	When I am rich I am still down to earth and authentically humble and sweet
If I'm rich I'm better than other people	I got rich because I learned something that other people didn't know, and have some great fortune that other people have had, but I am no better than anyone
It's better to give than to receive	Is blessed to receive with great gratitude the abundance of the world
Being rich makes people stingy	Because I am rich I am able to help less fortunate people
I should give away what I don't need for my basic needs	I am a very generous and still have money left for glamorous lifestyle for myself. I deserve a better lifestyle, just because.
Money is the root of all evil.	The *love* of money is evil. Putting money before integrity is evil.

TRANSFORMATION EXPLORATION 30: CIRCLE OF EXCELLENCE

This is my all-time favorite process for getting motivated. It is easy and very powerful. I strongly recommend doing the Circle of Excellence before a job interview, presentation, or, any business appointment. But, that's not all. You should use it for any situation where you want to be more confident and poised, ergo, a blind date, or any first date.

1. *Circle of Excellence.* Imagine a circle on the floor right in front of you, big enough to step into. This is your special *circle of excellence.*

      a. What would your circle look like? Is it a solid color, or multiple colors? Does it sparkle? Is it whirling around like a kaleidoscope?

      b. Would you also like it to have a sound like a soft hum that indicates how powerful it is?

2. <u>Relive confidence</u>. Standing in front of your circle, go back in your memory to a time when you were very confident, abundantly confident. Pick a strong, vibrant memory, one that you will enjoy reliving. Perhaps you were accepting an award, or you just aced a sales presentation.

3. <u>Relive that moment.</u>

      a. See what you saw then.

      b. Picture the setting?

      c. Who was there?

      d. What were you wearing?

      e. What was your posture like?

      f. What were you hearing?

      g. Who was talking?

      h. Were you saying anything to yourself?

      i. How did you feel inside?

      j. Where in your body did you feel it?

      k. Bring your emotions to a higher level.

4. <u>Step into your circle</u>

      a. When that feeling of confidence is at its fullest, step into the circle, reliving those empowering feelings.

      b. Let that feeling overwhelm you. Let it flow from your powerful circle up through your body and through your head.

      c. Bring it back down through your body and anchor it again to your circle of excellence.

      d. Let the felling of confidence become a bright light spinning up and down through your body.

5. <u>Step off your circle</u>
   a. Let the feeling subside for a moment.
6. <u>Step back on</u> and feel the power once again. Step off again.
7. <u>Using the Circle of Excellence Anchor</u>
   a. Now think of a specific time in your future when you want to have that same feeling of confidence. (a business situation: asking for a raise, a job interview; romantic encounter, demanding a divorce.)
   b. See and hear what will be there just before you want to feel confident.
   c. The cue could be the boss's office door, sitting at your desk or across the kitchen table from a client/prospect, a coffee shop (date), the engine of the car starting, the seat belt alarm (cue for being productive and focused on priorities).
   d. Imagine that situation unfolding around you in the future with these confident feelings fully available to you.
8. <u>Linking</u>. As soon as those cues are clear in your mind, step back into the circle and let the powerful energy of your circle of excellence flow through your body again and again.
9. <u>Check results</u>. Now step off the circle again, leaving those confident feelings there in the circle.
   a. Outside the circle, think again of the upcoming event.
   b. You'll find you automatically recall those confident feelings.
   c. This means you've already pre-programmed yourself for that upcoming event.
   d. You're feeling better about it and it hasn't even happened yet.
   e. When it arrives, you'll find yourself naturally responding more confidently.
10. <u>Pick up anchor.</u> Imagine your circle of excellence shrinking to a few inches. Pick it up and put it in your pocket or bra, or

wherever. Know that it is there for you to use any time you want confidence.

Oh, how I wish I were there with you to walk you through this process. It would be so much more empowering. In fact, I can do this over the phone. If you're interested give me a call and we'll discuss how I can help.

TRANSFORMATION EXPLORATION 31: EXPOSE THE LIES

This wonderful exercise is adapted from the work of my "SHee-Ro", Lisa Nichols, Author of several books including my favorite, "No Matter What!" Lisa is authentic, down-to-earth, and inspiring. To me this makes her lovable. She has given me permission to share this exercise with you. Go deep.

1. You'll need a pencil and pen with a stack of lined paper
2. Using pencil, write down every lie you tell yourself in each area of your life.
   - Business
   - Finance
   - Love
   - Body
   - Spiritual and faith
3. Skip 4 lines after each lie.
4. Give yourself a couple of days to come up with more lies. If you are honest you will have more than one page. After you uncover all the lies
5. Write the truth in red pen. (Okay, blue will do). The truth is the hard part because you think you don't know the truth. But you do! It may not all come at once, but it is there. I am still discovering truths. It never stops.

6. Spend 3 days reading the lies and the truth. By doing that, your mind will automatically go to the truth.

7. Then, erase the lie. Hopefully, you remembered to put it in pencil or you will need whiteout.

Voila! You have a new reality! Pretty cool, huh? I'll bet you made some real discoveries and it ain't over yet baby. You can use this exercise next year to expose more lies. In reality the lies are the representations we formed about our experiences.

Do you love yourself a little more now? You should. All that trash you told yourself about how you were 'not enough' was lies. You are just like the rest of us, full of foibles and fears, pimples and cellulite. Love yourself now, just as you are.

TRANSFORMATION EXPLORATION 32: MOUNTAIN EXERCISE:

My students love this exercise. Best done with colored pens or pencils.

I adore Lisa Nichols. She is an inspiring role model. One of the exercises she suggests is this:

Draw a mountain. It represents the climb to success. I recommend you draw it in color.

1. Under/in the mountain, place all your obstacles, beliefs, reasons and excuses for what is preventing you from accomplishing your goal, all the reasons you can't succeed. "I don't have babysitting, no money, no time, too dumb, fear of success, procrastination". These are the things you need to overcome.

2. In the sky or on top of the mountain, list all the things you will get when you break through all the obstacles

and beliefs that block you. 'Vacation, Pride, College for Johnny, Self-fulfillment"

3. Place yourself on the mountain. You may be half way up the mountain and still climbing. I decided, that even though I was not at the top of my mountain, I saw myself there so that is where I placed me. Do what feels right to you.

TRANSFORMATION EXPLORATION 33: Six-Step Neurological Alignment

This final process will bring everything you've done so far into crystal clarity. The purpose of the systemic alignment process is to align your physical self, mental self, social self, your emotional and spiritual selves with your higher purpose and mission. It will help ensure you are congruent in your goal.

For example, a single woman thinking about her work at these different levels:

Environmental: *"This women's group is a good place to showcase my product."*

Behavior: *"I need to make 20 calls a day to generate leads. I need to present my product/service to 10 women a month."*

Capability: *"I have good presentation skills. I need to master closing the sale."*

Belief: *"I believe I can be a top producer in my field. People like and trust me. I value selling people what they need."*

Step 1. Chose a goal...

Step 2. Review what achieving the goal will get for you. (The highest-level benefit)

Step 3.: Create anchors

Neurological Levels of Change

Stepping onto each space anchor, answer the appropriate question.

1. ENVIRONMENT	*"**Where** and **when** do I want to have this? Who are the other people I will interact with?"*
2. BEHAVIOR	*"What do I need to do? What are the specific actions I need to carry out, regardless of my capability?"*
3. CAPABILITIES	*"**How** will I carry out those behaviors?" "What capabilities do I have and which ones do I need to develop, to accomplish the goal."*
4. BELIEFS AND VALUES	*"**What** do I need to do in order to fulfill my goal? **What values** are important to me in achieving this goal? Will any of my values be violated? Beliefs can be both permissions and limitations.*
5. IDENTITY	*"**Who am I** when I have this goal? What **metaphor** represents the kind of person I am in this role." This is my basic sense of self, my core values and mission in life.*
6. SPIRITUAL	*"**Who am I serving?** What is the **vision** I am pursuing? My higher purpose?"*

Reverse Neurological Levels of Change
Step onto each space anchor in reverse order

6. SPIRITUAL	*Holding the state you entered into in the **Spiritual** space, take that physiology and inner experience and stop back into the **Identity** space.*
5. IDENTITY	*Experience the feeling of the **Spiritual** state as you think about **Identity.** Notice how it enriches the experience of the identity space.*
4. BELIEFS AND VALUES	*Take your experience of both your **Vision/ Mission** and your **Identity** and bring them into your **Beliefs and Values** space. Notice how it enhances and enriches your initial experience of your beliefs and values.*
3. CAPABILITIES	*Bring your **Vision, Identity, Beliefs, Values** into your **Capabilities** space. Experience how they strengthen, change, or enrich the capabilities you experience within yourself.*
2. BEHAVIOR	Bring your **Vision, Identity, Beliefs, Values** and **Capabilities** with you as you step into the **Behavior** space. Notice how even the most insignificant seeming behaviors are reflections and manifestations of all the higher levels within you.

| 1. ENVIRONMENT | Bring all levels of yourself into the **Environment** space and experience how it is transformed and enriched. |

TRANSFORMATION EXPLORATION 34: MASTER SELF TALK - AFFIRMATIONS:-DECLARATIONS-MANTRAS

Thoughts become even more powerful when verbalized. In fact, there is a direct correlation between the words that you use and the life you have. This is especially true of the things we tell ourselves.

Guided Self-talk, affirmations or declarations are the flip side of Visualization. You might say, visualization impacts the right brain, the creative side. Affirmations impact the left, logical, hemisphere of the brain. The idea of delineation of tasks between the left and right brain is not just an idea people have thrown around – it's backed up by scientific proof. American neuropsychologist Roger Sperry won the 1981 Nobel Prize in Physiology and Medicine for his work in split-brain research.

We all talk to ourselves, mostly silently. Only what we say to ourselves is negative. "Well, you screwed that up, again." "He'll never be interested in me." We want to create a new dialog for our auditory brain. One that is positive, inspiring, and encouraging. Imagine what can happen when you begin hearing, "You can do it!" Or, better yet, "I can do it!' "I can easily maintain my ideal weight and be fit and healthy." At first it is just lies. But, you know what happens if you lie to yourself often enough? You begin to believe it. Even an unintentional lie, or stories we tell ourselves can become truth to us. Like my husbands 400-pound Marlin. Each time he relieved catching the 'big one' his strong emotions made the fish seem bigger and bigger. Finally, it was 800-pounds. He really believed it! I had to reel him in before it became Moby Dick.

It is most natural to speak in negative sentences. "Don't worry." "Don't think about it." What if I said, "Don't think about a black bear." What do you instantly see in your mind's eye? A black bear. That is exactly what happens when we hear, "Don't worry about it." Our brain doesn't recognize negative language. To know what NOT to think about, we must first make a picture of what to think about. So, if we say to ourselves, "I don't want to be fat." Guess what our brain sees, our fat body. If we say, "I won't drink today." The mind ignores the 'won't'. This is the 'linguistic' part of NLP. So, instead of using negative language, use positive words. Instead of, "I won't worry about this." Rephrase it to, "I'm moving toward a solution." Or "I'm optimistic that an opportunity to fix my issue is close at hand." In other words, speak what you want to have happen.

The operation of developing your positive 'self-talk' simply expresses your goals. First, be sure your goals are: value based, clarified in great detail, have timelines, aligned with your passion and purpose, and congruent? So, the process is simple.

1. Take each of your goals
2. Create an encouraging statement about it. "I am becoming more confident each day."
3. Make sure the statement imparts possibilities. "I can easily maintain my fit, trim body."
4. Make it positive: "When I'm earning $5,000 a month I enjoy sharing it."
5. You can make some of them present tense, if you believe it. "I enjoy life's challenges, and I learn from everything that happens in my life."
6. Write it down. Create 3x5 cards and put them on the vanity to read in the morning. Put another set on the night stand to read before going to sleep.
7. Repeat often

Here are 60 sample affirmations. They are only ideas to get your own creative juices going.

1. I am resourceful – I have the ability to do whatever it takes to succeed, and to support my loved ones.
2. I enjoy life's challenges, and I learn from everything that happens in my life.
3. I live each day with passion and power!
4. I am growing more confident in my talents and abilities
5. I forgive myself and others easily
6. My confidence is unshakable because I live with integrity
7. I enjoy unlimited financial success
8. I was born to share freely in the abundance of life
9. I have much to give and I shared freely with others each and every day
10. My work is a great contribution to others, and I am richly rewarded for it
11. I am able to attract enjoy greater financial abundance each day
12. My gratitude opens me up to unlimited financials success
13. I can handle investment money wisely and I profit daily.
14. I deeply respect my body and take excellent care of it each day
15. I consistently think healthy thoughts
16. I am mastering the habit of proper breathing, and it gives me great energy.
17. I feel great pleasure from the health and strength of my physical body
18. I consume only wholesome foods and beverages.
19. I wake up each day feeling refreshed and vibrant, eager to start my day.
20. I respect my body healing wisdom and its energy.
21. I expect tol always feel and look young and healthy.
22. I retire each night feeling grateful for my vibrant health and energy.

23. I feel great pleasure as I take massive action to accomplish my goals

24. There is plenty of time to accomplish all I need to do.

25. I am a "do it now!" Person, and I make my time served me

26. I enjoy greater and greater success because I take consistent action to achieve my goals

27. I feel great freedom and pleasure as I get into action each day

28. I have resilient health. No matter what happens I just bounce back.

29. It's a treat to have delicious, healthy choices available to me in restaurants.

30. I choose to pass on the second piece of French bread and choose to enjoy the conversation instead.

31. When I dine out I take advantage of the opportunity to have fancy and healthy meals prepared for me.

32. It feels great to exercise and improve my flexibility and alertness

33. I plan how I can continue exercising as I travel

34. I easily maintain a fit, trim and healthy body

35. I prefer to eat healthy foods - my favorite foods are leafy green vegetables

36. I take advantage of a fine chef to prepare a healthy meal for me when I travel

37. I stay at four and five-star hotels and love to go to the exercise room to work out

38. When I am hungry I put my hand on my stomach and realized it is just a physical sensation

39. Before I eat I connect with my body and with my higher spirit and request that I be notified when I'm 80% full

40. I am grateful and happy that I can travel first class 30 days a year- where ever I want, with whom I want, and stay as long as I want

41. I am happy and grateful that I am living in beautiful surroundings, with luxurious furnishings

42. I travel 1ˢᵗ class for business. I can feel myself sitting in that first-class luxurious seat sipping water and eating healthy snacks working on my iPad or reading a fabulous book

43. I am free of all cravings for alcohol and drugs

44. I speak only kind positive words to make people feel happy

45. I am a positive role model for women including my daughters

46. I I am living the life of my dreams because I persevered no matter what

47. I am touching the lives of thousands of women

48. Everyone in my niche wants to hire me

49. I am the solution to the problem she most wants solved

50. Everyone in my niche loves me, I am loved, deeply loved.

51. Everyone in my niches wants to be my friend

52. My niche is opening to my deeper work

53. Within my niche endless possibilities are available to me

54. I am thrilled that new women are joining my tribe daily

55. I am grateful that I get to follow my passion and that I have found my divine purpose in life.

56. I am eternally grateful for my daughter and sisters.

57. I associate with wealthy successful people like myself and I am comfortable and authentic in their presence. They are just like me.

58. I am generous I am giving, especially now that I have so much to give I donate to various charities.

59. I am now earning $100,000 a year and more.

60. I allow my higher consciousness to bring me answers to my most pressing questions.

Set intention for today

- On three 3x5 cards, write down three intentions to accomplish by the end of the day that will make you feel really good and that you really accomplished something.
- Right down some actions you will take for each one

- Example: Intention- Be fit and trim
  - o Use less salt
  - o Drink more water
  - o Exercise so many minutes
  - o Stretch
  - o Remember to breathe throughout the day
  - o Take breaks
  - o Eat every two hours
- Set one personal intention for the day
  - o Only say nice things. Express happy thoughts
  - o Remember people do not want to hear complaining griping and misery
  - o People do not want to be advised or criticized
  - o Look in the mirror and state "3 things I am grateful for today."
- List 3 things you forgive yourself for
- List what you will commit to today

Now have a terrific day!!!

TRANSFORMATION EXPLORATION 35: DYNAMIC SPIN

This is a relatively new process created by my NLP mentors, Internationally renowned trainers, Tim and Kris Hallbum. It is very effective at changing negative self-talk, among other things.

1. Think about a recurring negative message that plays over and over in your head, or a situation where you are not as resourceful as you'd like to be.
2. Is it a 'you' message, "Oh, you're so stupid." or an 'I' message? "I could never do that."
3. Whose voice is it? For instance, Mother told me, "Get your head out of the clouds. You're not special." My client Tracy

needed a more resourceful way to respond when her father verbally abused her.

4. Where is it coming from? Does it seem to be coming from the back of your head, or perhaps, in your left ear? Tracy's was in her head.

5. When you think about the message, where do you feel it in your body? Tracy had violent physical reactions, her fist clenched, shoulders hunched up toward her ears, jaw clenched, which left her with a terrible head ache.

6. Take the message or feeling and place it in front of you, maybe 10 feet or so. Suspend it at eye level. Let it just levitate there.

7. Turn it into an object that is a metaphor for the message. (a dagger, brick, etc.) Don't over think it, whatever comes up is right, even if it seems stupid. And, it can change. Tracy was surprised to see a black cloud when she thought about her father belittling her. (Note: Do not use a person as the metaphor. If a person comes to mind, simply find a metaphor for the person.)

8. Now, let the object begin to spin or rotate in whatever direction it wants to go. If it's not rotating, just imagine that it is. It may even change forms. As Tracy's black cloud began to spin it turned into a black tornado. It seemed so appropriate for her father's tirades.

9. STOP its rotation. Ask the object. "What is your positive intent?" Tracy decided that her body was going into fight or flight mode, to keep her from speaking-up and causing the tirade to escalate. Mind you, Tracy is 54 and her father is 76.

10. Now, spin it in the opposite direction. Let it spin faster and faster until it disintegrates into a million tiny specks of dust and flows into the cosmos.

11. Imagine the particles are circulating in the universe gathering all the knowledge and wisdom of the 'collective consciousness'. All the wisdom from the greatest minds of all time.

12. Now, let a new metaphor or gift appear. Sometimes clients get a gift-wrapped box. If that happens, open the box and find the gift inside. This new metaphor represents the true message and it's positive intent. Tracy got the Christian Fish Symbol.

13. You will know the positive intent of the message. Mother didn't want me to be heart-broken because she didn't believe it was possible for me to have my dream. She was protecting me. The behavior came from love. Tracy's new message was, "I don't have to put up with anybody's shit anymore! I am loved and lovable."

14. With both hands, bring that new symbol into your heart and breathe deeply allowing the new statement to flow through your body making you feel very loved. Very worthy.

15. You now have a new reality. I'd love to hear about your experience with this.

SUMMARY:

I'll bet you tell yourself things that you would never say to another person. And, the more you say them, or think them, the more they become who you are. Why not write the script for your life starting with positive affirmations.? It's okay, if in the beginning, you think they are lies. If you lie to yourself long enough, you'll believe it!

KEY #10

NEVER GIVE UP

"The secret to success without perseverance remains a secret."

~Carole Rose

Ah, we've made it to the final step in my formula for success, which, coincidentally, is also the fifth key to achieving anything your want - Perseverance. This is not as hard as you may think. It's not like sticking to a diet. In that case, you are always sacrificing something yummy for something not very thrilling. When you are following your dream, you are sacrificing something that is less enjoyable, (the life you have) for something that is thrilling (your passion). Still, the road will not be without speedbumps and potholes. You must keep constant vigil for the people and thoughts that can send you careening off the cliff. Let's examine our biggest fears associated with going for it.

<u>Risk</u>

Wouldn't life be wonderful if there was absolutely no risk in anything we did or said? We could walk up to anyone and tell them exactly what we think of them, with no negative ramifications to worry about. We could skydive and bungee jump to our hearts content and never concern ourselves with a parachute not opening or the cord breaking. We could start a new business and have no concerns whatsoever that we might fail. We could love without fear of rejection. Wouldn't life be great? Maybe.

Risk can be defined as the intentional interaction with uncertainty. It assumes some negative consequences if you fail. Yet, taking risks is necessary to our growth. What if you never tried anything new? You wouldn't be driving a car. You couldn't fall in love because there is far too much uncertainty there. If we were born with the fear of risk, we would never walk.

The fear of taking a risk can be as innocuous as trying roller skating, or so excruciating it will keep a person housebound (Agoraphobia). We take risk everyday simply by living.

Some of us are risk junkies -Evel Knievel. Some of us are afraid of our own shadow. Well-adjusted people are in the middle. After all, what would life be like if we took no risks? Boring, comes to mind. And, lonely. Being satisfied with who we have become, instead of claiming the woman we were meant to be. We can't expand our horizons if we don't take risks, and that means overpowering the twin dragons- Fear and Doubt.

Not taking any risks keeps you playing small. Taking risks then can lead us to our greatest achievements. But it can also lead us to failure, destruction, catastrophe and when taken to the extreme, even death. And that is why successful people always balance risk against reward. They don't make snap judgments whenever there is an element of risk to their decisions. They weigh the pros against the cons and then take what is considered a calculated risk. And it is always weighted towards the upside.

To live life well, you must quell the fear of failure and the fear of rejection. You must learn to trust yourself and others. I didn't say 'eliminate fear', just learn to move forward despite it. As we speakers say, "You don't get rid of the butterflies, you just teach them to fly in formation.

> "Children have a lesson adults should learn, to not be ashamed of failing, but to get up and try again. Most of us adults are so afraid, so cautious, so 'safe,' and therefore so shrinking and rigid and afraid that it is why so many humans fail. Most middle-aged adults have resigned themselves to failure." ~ Malcolm X

Failure

Many of us grew up believing that failing and making mistakes are the worst things that can happen to us. We may grow up thinking that if we fail we are losers and that people will laugh at us or will look down on us. Believe me, I've got this lesson. I have looked like a fool many times in the eyes of my family and friends. And, the public. Many of my early speeches bombed. I was embarrassed and couldn't wait to leave the room. But, I did it again, and again, until I didn't look like a rank amateur. It can hurt. I must say, no one in my family ever failed, except my Dad, who failed constantly. But, no one else ever tried anything. They played it safe and got jobs they were sure they could not fail at. Yes, Dad and I were the only fools on the family tree. We were entrepreneurs and entrepreneurs become very familiar with failure. We were both considered pipe-dreamers, and, I'm sure, sometimes flakey.

Sometimes when you're disappointed because you did not achieve your desired outcome, your first thought is: "I shouldn't have tried. What made me think I could do this, I am a fool!" You are not a fool. You are not a failure. Failure is a thing that happens to you, it isn't who you are, any more than being rich or poor is who you are. You are the same wonderful person you identified in the chapter on values. But the truth is, failure can make us feel bad about ourselves. "Can', because it doesn't have to, not when you accept it for the learning lesson it is. What did Edison say when his light bulb failed 9999 times? "I haven't failed. I've found 9,999 ways it doesn't work." Source Brainy Quotes

Successful people lick their wounds and try again. I mean that. I have felt such despair that I laid in my tub in a fetal position wailing for hours. The next day, I shook it off and looked for a new plan.

In her inspiring book, 'Esteemable Acts', Francine Ward said this,

"Every time I failed the California Bar exam a piece of me died. I saw each failure as one more reason to feel worthless. Finally, standing at the door of despair yet one more time, I came to appreciate the gift I had been given: the gift of myself. Failing the California Bar Exam repeatedly was the single most painful experience of my life, but it was the one that has provided me with the greatest opportunities. I didn't like it when it was happening, but years later I came to understand that it was all part of a master plan. I needed to learn the lesson of surrender- not giving up, but letting go."

Sometimes we are insistent on having something that the Universe has not intended. In 2013, I went back into real estate sales, thinking I would be a super-star again. I still had my Broker's license, I was exceptional at selling, and I had done it before. I should have been an overnight success like I was in the previous two real estate sales careers, right? I went a full year without one sale. I was embarrassed, humiliated and ashamed. I wanted to hideout and clean house for the rest of my life, take no risk. That lasted about 2 weeks. That career was not in my divine plan. I had to surrender to the fact that there was something else I was supposed to do. I had to go back to fulfilling my purpose. Even though I was challenged with enumerable obstacles in my coaching career, that had prevented me from making a living at it, I knew I had to find a way to share my gift. When I committed to follow my passion, no matter what, I began to see what I needed to do differently. It was time for this book and get on the speaking circuit.

Adversity and set-backs

The question isn't whether or not we will have setbacks, disappointments, and failures in business and in life – we will. Rather, the question is, how will we deal with them? Will we become upset, immobilized, frustrated, hopeless, or pessimistic? Or will we take a more positive approach?

Most setbacks are nothing more than small stuff disguised as big stuff. In other words, it can seem significant, even insurmountable in the moment. Yet, once we get through them we look back on setbacks and even failures as speedbumps or detours, rather than road blocks. Adversity, no matter how awful, may even advance your success. Several women have told me that being forced to file for bankruptcy was the best thing that ever happened to them. Sure, it was painful while it was happening, but it woke them up and taught them some important lessons.

We can't control the universe

In 1980 mortgage interest rates soured to 24%. The entire real estate industry came to a screeching halt. I got a call a week from an associate who wanted me to join Amway. In 2007, we went into the biggest economic downturn since 1930. Hiring a coach was not in the budget for most women. In fact, coaches were flocking to MLMs (Multi-level Marketing) and trying to recruit each other. It was pretty discouraging to pay $50 for a networking dinner, only to be cross-recruiting. I tried a few MLMs myself, and failed. Were all these Realtors and Coaches failures? Of course not. However, some Realtors and network marketers still made a living. You may have been making great money owning a video store, then came DVDs, and then DVRs. You could own a taxi, then along came Uber. The above are called economic obsolescence. No amount of positive thinking is going to alter the fact that you no longer have a saleable product. People get catastrophic illnesses, or lose limbs. Women get divorced. Hey, shit happens. And, sometimes, it rains on everyone's parade.

What can you do when adversity strikes? First, accept it. Don't do like so many entrepreneurs do, and go into debt trying to salvage a doomed business. I know many contractors who lost their home that way in the 2008 recession. Sometimes, you need to give up sooner, rather than later. Second, realize that this is an opportunity to change direction. It could mean; find a new passion, or perhaps just a new avenue to achieve your purpose. We get locked into thinking there is only one way to manifest our dream. I have seen proof that when one door closes, another one, even better, opens. However, if you don't release the fear, your subconscious cannot go to work finding the door. It's time to exercise some faith. It's time to meditate, visualize and keep an open mind.

Third, understand that this is only temporary. Recessions pass, injuries heal, hearts heal after losing a loved one. Stop asking the wrong questions. Instead of asking, "Why me?" Ask empowering questions, "What lesson am I supposed to learn from this?" Where's the opportunity lying inside the adversity?"

How do you know when to give up?

That's a question only you can answer. Have you tried everything you can think of? Have you hired the right coaches? Have you run out of resources, cash, energy? Is it something beyond your control? Is it ruining some other aspect of your life? Remember, I tenaciously hung onto my coaching career, even when I was losing our life savings trying; even when it was making John unhappy. I didn't realize that an outside force, the economy, was working against me. That was my time to give it up, or at least take a break. Now, I realize, it wasn't that I should give up on my purpose of helping women, it was that, I needed a new vehicle to do it. Sometimes, it's that simple. I got stuck in the wrong method to share my gift. I couldn't see it at the time. I just kept hitting that brick wall and trying to knock it down. So, perhaps, it's time to find a new way to share your gift.

I know, you're busy. You get home late from work and have to cook and do laundry and help the kids with homework. You barely have time to take a bubble bath. Now, a male coach might say, "Those are just excuses! Get over it." Not Aunt Carole. You can only do so much without having a breakdown. You need to be a mommy while you can, if you can. You can't put the kids (that are already born) on hold until you build your career. But, you can put your career on hold until the kids are in school. I put my career on hold so John could have his dream. I have no regrets. He got to be a success because of me. That was reward in itself. I do hope, you can do something every day to keep your passion alive. You could spend a few minutes at lunch surfing the web for ideas from your competition. You can make vision boards with the kids. Look at and vividly imagine your dreams. Before you know it, something unexpected will happen to make it possible for you to follow your dream sooner than you thought. That's the power of the 'Law of Attraction'.

Of course, you could be pursuing the wrong goal. At the encouragement of her husband, Jenett pursued a certificate in phlebotomy (drawing blood). She tried so hard and had to take one class three times. She dreaded sticking needles into people. Naturally, she felt like a failure. I always knew phlebotomy had nothing to do with her passion and purpose of helping women, but hubby thought she would have a steady income, so she should buckle down and complete the course. I don't care how smart you are, you can't force yourself to be great at something you are not interested in. John and I took a course to become Certified Remodeling Contractors. It was a cake-walk for him. Not for me. I couldn't get the algebra and I barely knew a reciprocating saw from a hammer. It was very frustrating. I felt stupid, just as Jenett had.

I hope that after doing the work on finding your passion and purpose, you are not going to fall for just getting a J.O.B. to make a living. It's your birthright to pursue your dream, if, it doesn't hurt someone else. So, it's not so much, giving up, as it is finding the right path to fulfill your dream. Let's look at some obstacles that can trick you into thinking you need to give up.

<u>The Panic Point</u>

Sometimes, on the verge of success, you begin to experience some unexplainable fear that seems to take control of your life. The paralyzing fear is so strong, you become debilitated. You may feel like you're having a nervous breakdown. You cry. You want to crawl under the covers and hide out. It can destroy you if you don't understand what is happening.

It's called 'The Panic Point' and it has wreaked havoc on my life. It is the most lethal tool the ego has in its arsenal to keep you from claiming the woman you are meant to be. Remember, it's the responsibility of the unconscious mind to keep us safe, to keep our body in balance, to keep us comfortable. If our temperature goes above 98.6 we get a fever to cool us down. If we are cold, we shiver to warm us. If our blood sugar gets out of range, the unconscious releases insulin to regulate it. This homeostasis as best.

In the same way, the subconscious makes us act consistent with our subconscious goals, values and expectations. So, if you have an unconscious fear that if you get rich you'll turn into an amoral, unscrupulous being, the unconscious springs into action to protect you. STOP! DANGER AHEAD! It has an arsenal of tools and tricks to get you back to your comfort zone.

When EGO believes it is not safe to get rich or fall in love, the effects are devastating. And, the further you venture outside your egos' comfort zone, the more desperate she becomes, and the deadlier the tools she uses to save you. First, the warning. She shouts, "Danger! You're going to get hurt!" What your soul hears is:

> "Who do you think you are anyway?"
> "This isn't for you, you can't do this."
> "You don't have what it takes."
> "You don't deserve it."
> "You'll never amount to anything so why bother."
> "Pipe dreamer! Pollyanna!"
> "You're not good enough at what you do."
> "You need more training.

Here 11 signs to watch out for:

1. You're too busy. There is no extra time in a woman's life. It's about priorities.
2. You're scared into inaction. "Omygawd, what if…?
3. You can't make decisions. You want others to tell you what to do.
4. You lose interest. On the brink of success, you change paths. "I should be doing this instead." The grass is greener.
5. You're forgetful. I would miss appointments or forget to take the paperwork.
6. You're disorganized. You wait until the last minute to print the proposal, and the printer jams. You can't find your car keys.

7. You fog up, space out. Confusion is a by-product of stress.
8. You feel paralyzed. "I just can't think or get going."
9. You find reasons not to act. "I can't, because..." "I can't leave my kids."
10. You're impatient. "This is taking way too long."
11. You keep running into naysayers. Other people say, "You can't do that." "That's not possible."

If you don't heed the warning, Ego springs into action to keep you safe! And, the more important the goal or vision is to your soul's evolution, the more resistance you will encounter when you pursue it.

> "The danger is greatest when the finish line is in sight. Resistance knows we›re about to beat it. It hits the panic button. It marshals one last assault and slams us with everything it›s got. Be wary at the end."
> -Steven Pressfield

When your resistance to change, your resistance to claiming the woman we are meant to be, tries to overpower you, the ego seems to conspire with the universe stop you. Resistance can also show up in these surprising ways.

- <u>Technology breaks down:</u> I've had this happen several times while preparing for a big sale. It seems to be 'Carole's Law', that when you wait until the last hour to print the paperwork, the printer breaks down. Thus, I would arrive late for the presentation with my poise and confidence shattered. I would know going in that I was not going to get the sale.
- <u>Physical breakdowns</u>: Oh yes, the subconscious can make you physically ill to take you out. I'm sure that is why I got cancer. I wanted to escape from working with John. Remember, I even claimed it. "John, you are going to give me

cancer." You can make yourself sick. Maybe just a bad cold or an eye infection. My friend got laryngitis when she was about to speak to 1000 women. Or, you could be knocked on your ass by symptoms that imitate the flu. Denis Waitley, Psychologist to the astronauts, said he has seen proof that mental obsessions can lead to physical manifestations.

- <u>Blowing sales</u>. For me that shows up as: Saying the wrong things, not asking for the sale, losing rapport with the prospects, showing up late, being unprepared, not following up on leads, making stupid mistakes on paperwork or financial details. Really bad!

- <u>Making poor financial decisions.</u> This could be not collecting money owed you or selling something to some flake who refuses to pay. It could be missing payments, so your credit gets screwed up. Bouncing checks which causes a whirlwind of bad check charges which causes more checks to bounce. It's a vicious cycle that buries you.

- <u>Accidents.</u> The ego can cause you to take your eyes off the road for just long enough to plow into someone, or to slip on a banana peel. It is very clever. Who can say just why they 'accidentally' lost their wallet with the rent money in it. The Universe works in strange ways.

- <u>Mechanical failures</u>: The transmission goes out. "How can I work without a car?" You must spend the business budget on a new frig.

- <u>Procrastinating.</u> When I signed a contract for over $300,000 a year as a Sales Trainer and Recruiter, I spent 3 months rewriting my program, the program that had earned me acclaim and got me hired for this amazing job in the first place. I got fired.

- <u>Relationships become challenging</u>. At one point in my professional career I imagined that my boss was trying to cheat me out of money I had earned. It was all a misunderstanding, but, in my distorted fear of success, it was real. I stubbornly walked away from the job, and a very special friendship. It's not uncommon to experience turmoil in our love life when we are claiming the woman we were meant to be. Our loved one may feel threatened, or perhaps, due to the stress, our disposition is not as sweet as it once was. Going for the gold requires self-care. If you overwork so you can rush forward, it may have the opposite result. Burn-out can knock you on your ass and you will lose more time than you thought you saved.

- <u>You begin to blame others irrationally</u>. Oh yes! Blame your spouse, your boss, the webmaster. I call myself on if, "Oh, there I go with the blame game."
- <u>You blame outside forces</u>. "It's the economy, terrorism, an earthquake." (That was a good one, don't you think?)
- <u>Money issues</u>. The car breaks down, the dryer goes on the blink. You just can't afford to keep moving forward.

"If you hear a voice say, 'you cannot paint', by all means, paint and that voice will be silenced." Vincent Van Gogh

<u>Crossing 'The Panic Point'</u>

The only way to claim the woman you are meant to be, is by crossing over the panic point. This is when most women drop out. They don't want to pay the price, go through pain of change. We are always avoiding pain. That's why we must be so diligent in visualizing the outcome, seeing ourselves as the woman we want to be. Let's face it, if the panic point didn't exist, everyone would be wildly successful. You are being asked to stretch beyond your comfort zone, and most women avoid discomfort like the plague. Our first instinct is to 'self-medicate'. What is your poison of choice?

- TV, drugs, potato chips, alcohol, gossip, shopping, sweets, smoking, pigging out, gambling, over work, crawling under the covers, or…..
- Meditation, visualization, affirmations, soaking in a tub of lavender salts, listening to music, dancing, shopping (okay, this is on both list because it is good therapy, if, you don't overspend), call your mentor

Here's a very important point- the Panic Point is always strongest the 1st time. Then, it becomes a game you recognize and want to play. "Oh, I must be heading for another big breakthrough. Okay, bring it on!" Are you willing to endure short-term discomfort for long-term success? How badly do you want success? To get your quantum leap you must be comfortable with being uncomfortable for a while. That's when the big money and big opportunities appear. Be willing to feel what you haven't wanted to feel, until the ego retreats. Don't allow yourself to go to the dark side and get negative. You know what that energy attracts and how it can block your vision. You start believing in your failure and the RAS only sees more proof that you are right. You fail to see opportunity for your breakthrough and you stay stuck. Often opportunity shows up as a misfortune. It's painful at the moment, but there is a bigger plan. It may seem like pointless chaos but look deeper, the universe is rearranging itself.

<u>Give in to self-pity</u>

When you're down in the valley and you feel hopeless and helpless, it's hard to bootstrap yourself out of it. Sometimes we just need to wallow in the valley. I say that is perfectly okay. Eat chocolate all day, cry, indulge in self-pity if you want. Just don't put down roots in the valley. Personally, after my one-day pity-party, I am back in control. I just pick up the pieces and move on or start over.

Remember, failure is not permanent. It is a stepping stone. Francine Ward explained it this way,

> *"Failure is not fun, and it can even be debilitating at times. It can rob you of your spirit and your will to keep going. But the key to getting through a disappointing experience is not to give it more power than it deserves. Failure is temporary. Indeed, the slap to your ego will linger for a while, but eventually you'll forget the intensity of the pain you once held so dear. My advice: Get up, dust yourself off, and start all over again."*

<u>What to do when you have failed?</u>

1. Give yourself 1000 2nd chances. Some people study for years and spend thousands of dollars getting a degree in business. Entrepreneurs learn on the job. This is our 'degree'. It will cost money and take time. Give yourself the compassion that you would give a stranger.

2. Don't keep score- stop tracking all the things that didn't work. Remember, what you focus on, grows. The power lies in getting back up when you're knocked down. I'll bet you can't name one successful person who has not had the wind knocked out of their sales.

3. Future pace- Focus on how it will *feel* when you make it.

4. Self-care – Take a "me" break. Get a massage, go to the park, call your sister. We women get caught up in taking care of everyone but ourselves. You'll burn out quick if you don't take care of yourself first.

5. Maintain an optimal energy level. Get more rest. Eat better. Ask your body what it needs.

6. Remind yourself of the woman you are becoming, and that this is just Ego trying to keep you small.

There will most assuredly be obstacles. Don't allow yourself to see them as road blocks. Instead, see them as speed bumps. Slow down and get your grip back and then move on cautiously. It's normal to get down occasionally. And, when it happens, it can seem hopeless. But, it isn't. Or, rather it doesn't have to be, unless you give up. You are creating your destiny with every thought you allow to linger. Speak positive, even when you're feeling down.

TRANSFORMATION EXPLORATION 36: MY LESSON FROM FAILURE

Have you ever felt the sting of failure? Have you felt the embarrassment or even shame of it? Take a moment to relive that experience. As painful as it was, you survived and are not scarred for life, right? So, ask yourself:

- What lesson came out of the failure?
- Did you move on to something more valuable in your life as a result of the failure?

TRANSFORMATION EXPLORATION 37: SUCCESS LIST

You've accomplished many things in your life. Things you never even thought of as successes. Make a list of everything you can think of going back to birth. Start it with, "I'm proud that I …..i.e.
1. Learned to walk without being able to crawl (you can't crawl with one arm)
2. Founded the 'Four Leaf Clover Club' when I was 8. List everything you can think of. It is encouraging and inspiring.
3. Then share with 2 people.

TRANSFORMATION EXPLORATION 38: WRITE TWO LETTERS TO YOURSELF

1. Love letter to myself.

Dear Carole,

I am so glad I am you. You are an awesome woman. I know you don't see it in yourself, but others do. You constantly underrate yourself and put yourself down.

I love you. I love your brilliance, radiance, kindness and generosity. I love that you cry with compassion for others. I love what you have done for John's kids.

You have been a God-send to John. I love you for making him feel good about himself, worthy, loved, confident, creative. I love you for being faithful and giving.

Carole, you are special. Pat and Jeanie love you. Uncle Rusty loves you and many others love you. Women want to be like you. You are a role model. Sure, you feel you let them down by not being able to solve everyone's problems, but you can't fix the world.

You are talented and self-determined. I love that you are sweet natured.

Give yourself credit.

All my love,
Carole

2. Thank you letter

Date it one year from today.

Dearest brave, persevering Carole.

Hurray for you!! Woo-Hoo!!!! You did it!!! Thank you for not giving up. When it looked so bleak and you felt so hopeless.

Thank you for honoring John along the way by cutting way back on business expenses so you could stay in business long enough to find the missing link. Bless him for not killing you for investing over $150,000 to find the key.

Thank you, Carole, for understanding his fear when he yelled and criticized you and demanded you get a J-O-B at 67 years old. You handled it well.

Thank you, Carole, for believing in your dream when no one else did. Thank you for moving forward even when you doubted yourself.

Now, just look at you. Here you are the dynamic, slender, fit, awesome woman you were in 1979, only better- wiser, more grounded, more skilled, more authentic.

Thank you for making $_____ in the last 12 months and proving to everyone you could do it.

And, Carole, thank you for the spectacular vacation to the Keys with John. That was even better than we expected. The water was beautiful. It was so generous of you to take us out to eat and dance in the some of the best places in town. John caught the shark he had longed to catch. Wow, that was sure fun, watching him reel it in.

Carole, thank you for taking care of your body. You look fabulous and your energy shines through.

Thanks for being a great step-mother to John's kids and Grandmother to all 11 of our joint grandchildren.

Thank you for the flat screen TV for the new house, the atrium, hot tub, and all the grand furniture. Without your perseverance, stubbornness, tenacity and positive thinking, John and I would've lost our home and ended up living like the people I most want to help. Yikes!!

You are a wonderful woman- an inspiration and role model.

Lovingly,
Carole

"Vision without execution is hallucination." Thomas Edison

TAKE DECISIVE ACTION

"You don't need to see the whole staircase only the first step." Martin Luther King Jr.

Most people don't start until they know the 'how'. Don't worry about the how. Let your intuition guide you and move forward one step at a time. That step may trigger the next thing you need to do. Begin thinking, acting, speaking and being in accordance with your dream.

Let go of fear. It will paralyze you. When you decide you're going to have it, come hell or high water, the Universe will show you the way. Remember, if you doubt, you will see only obstacles. When you believe, you'll see opportunities. It's magical. Napoleon Hill calls this 'definiteness of purpose'. He calls those without it, 'drifters'. Drifters have no power to influence their life. They have no dream and simply meander through life as victims of circumstances. So, I ask you....

- Are you ready to stop playing small?
- How badly do you want it?

- Are you willing to persevere, even when others don't believe in you?
- Or will you retreat, continue to play small, wondering 'what if'?
- Learn to love being uncomfortable

"Most men lead lives of quiet desperation and go to the grave with the song still in them." —Henry David Thoreau

Don' forget, what we really want is the feeling. If you're doing what you love, you are contented. So, it's important to realize why you're doing it. Here is one of my favorite stories.

There was a big city businessman who once went on holiday to a faraway beach. One day he walked past a local fisherman who was lazing around, with his fishing rod in the water, enjoying the sun and a beer.

The city man's mind went to work immediately. The fishing spot was a gold mine, and a serious fishing business would thrive in the area. "Why are you so stupid?" he asked the fisherman. "Get some boats, hire some extra hands, and in a few years, you will turn your little shop into a million-dollar business!"

The local man asked him. "And what would you do once you have a million dollars?"

The city man stared back blankly. "Why, I would have so much free time I could sit around and fish all day."

"Success is never final; failure is never fatal." -Conrad Hilton

Choose your regret.

Twenty years from now, you may be more disappointed by the things that you didn't do, by the missed opportunities, than by the things you did do that didn't turn out so well. I hear it all the time. I should've bought that lot for $50k when I had the chance. Now it's worth $1Mil. I should've quit my job years ago. I should've left my husband, started a business, invested in myself. I 've never heard anyone say, "I wish I hadn't tried to succeed". And, that includes many entrepreneurs who didn't make it.

Commit

The final piece to the success quotient is to commit. You see, if you're just interested, you will do what is convenient and what is comfortable. You'll come up with stories and reasons why you can't. If you are committed, you will do whatever it takes. What is it they say? The chicken is interested, the egg is committed. When the Universe knows you are determined to get what you want, it will yield- if it is your true mission.

Summary:

Failure is never permanent. Success may be fleeting. Don't judge your life by what you have not achieved. Judge your life by the joy, love and fulfillment you created. That is what is really important.

CONCLUSION

Writing this book has been the hardest thing I have ever undertaken. Only you can judge whether the book is a success. I judge myself a success for finishing it. I worry that readers will see my lack of education in my grammar and misuse of semi-colons. I worry that I disclosed too much information about myself. But, then again, I know in my heart that this labor of love is for women who need to hear what I have said. If I can save one woman from a miserable destiny, I have served my mission in life. So, please let me know if I have helped you. I leave you with this.

<u>My prayer for you.</u>

This is my friend whom I love, and this is my prayer for her.

Help her live her life to the fullest. Show her how to shine her light so she can bless the world with the gifts you gave her.

Cause her to see opportunities, not obstacles.

Give her courage to persevere when the ego tries to keep her from being all she is meant to be.

Lift her up when she needs You the most, and

Let her trust that the desire deep within, is from you and you will help her have it.

Show her how to trust her own wisdom, and most of all,

Let her love herself a little more each and every day.

Amen!

Thank you bottom of my heart!

Hugs,

Aunt *Carole*

Carole

Printed in the United States
By Bookmasters